As Good as Gold *300 Years of British Bank Note Design*

Detail from the back of the £20 'D' showing the statue of Shakespeare from the Kent memorial in Westminster Abbey. Issued July 1970.

As Good as Gold

300 Years of British Bank Note Design

V. H. Hewitt and J. M. Keyworth

Published for the Trustees of the British Museum
by British Museum Publications
in association with the Bank of England

Back of the £10 'D' showing a portrait of Florence Nightingale and a scene in the barracks hospital at Scutari.

This book is dedicated to Elizabeth and Douglas Anderson
and to the memory of Olga Alexandra Dyball

© 1987 The Trustees of the British Museum and the Governor and Company of the Bank of England

Published by British Museum Publications Ltd, 46 Bloomsbury Street, London WC1B 3QQ
Designed by James Shurmer
Set in Apollo and printed by Jolly & Barber Ltd, Rugby, Warks.

Contents

Foreword

The publication of this book has been timed to coincide with the opening of a major exhibition of the same title at the British Museum. Although standing in its own right as a study of three centuries of British bank note design, the book is, nevertheless, complementary to the exhibition, exploring and explaining aspects of the history of bank notes in a depth which would not have been otherwise possible.

Both exhibition and book are the result of co-operation between two institutions of international repute; the fact that they have such vastly differing roles in the world has proved no bar to this co-operation which has undoubtedly been mutually beneficial and doubly so for the public.

Through the medium of book and exhibition the British Museum has performed two of its fundamental functions — those of increasing the fund of human knowledge and furthering the cause of scholarship, and has at the same time, celebrated the coming of age of its paper money collection. For its part, the Bank of England has, exceptionally, made hitherto unpublished material available from its museum collection. This enterprise well illustrates the richness and diversity of the source material from which today's notes are derived.

David M. Wilson

Director
The British Museum

R. Leigh-Pemberton

Governor
The Bank of England

Preface

The design of everyday objects which we take for granted often merits closer study for what it reveals both about the objects themselves and about popular taste. The design of bank notes is an excellent case in point. First and foremost it is dictated by the purpose of notes and how they are used: the issuing authority and amount of the note must be easily identified, and the design must be as difficult as possible to forge. Today the demands of security are paramount, but it is also desirable that bank notes are attractive to the public. Historically this has been extremely important, not least as a means of encouraging people to accept paper money when it was still a relatively unfamiliar form of currency. Changing fashions in the visual arts have had a clear influence on the development of bank note design.

This book is a survey of bank note design in Britain from the first notes of the seventeenth century to those of the present day. It is not a history of British banking, nor is it a catalogue of British bank notes. There already exist good examples of both, several of which are listed in the bibliography. We have, however, attempted to explain the reasons for changes in design, and this necessarily involves some discussion of banking history as well as economic and social conditions, and the commercial application of art as industrial design.

Technical aspects of note production – paper-making, engraving and printing – are touched upon insofar as they have determined, or themselves been affected by, changes in the design of notes. This is especially relevant in the nineteenth century, when engravers in London and the provinces experimented with innovative methods of security printing in order to prevent forgery.

As the title suggests, we have concentrated on notes issued in the British Isles – England, Scotland, Wales and Northern Ireland – but it would seem unreasonably chauvinistic to avoid those places which have close associations with Britain, historically or geographically. References to notes of the Irish Republic, the Isle of Man, and the Channel Isles have therefore been included where appropriate.

Obviously we can only describe and illustrate a fraction of the thousands of different notes issued in Britain over three centuries, but we hope we have conveyed something of their variety and charm. Ultimately the interest goes beyond the notes to what they show us about ourselves, the way we live now and the way we have lived in the past.

While final responsibility for the text and for any errors is ours alone, we are indebted to a number of institutions and individuals who have made valuable contributions to the production of this book. Nigel Bevitt-Smith of the Bank of England Printing Works has given unstinting support, making available important illustrative material. Richard Reed at the National Westminster Bank kindly provided a picture of an early note of Smiths of Nottingham. Much of the photography has been prepared especially for this publication, an exacting job splendidly carried out by ChaZ Howson, Nick Nicholls, Don Ford and John Deacon. The chore of proof-reading has been considerably lightened (for us) by the kind help of Derrick Byatt, Tony Carlisle and Barrie Cook. We are particularly grateful to Jane Thomas, who has patiently read the typescript several times in checking proofs and in the awesome task of compiling the index and to James Shurmer, the designer, for bringing it all together so well.

The interest of all our colleagues has been tremendously encouraging, as has the support of our families. We must give special thanks to Roger Hewitt and the Secretarial Unit of the Secretary's Division of the Bank of England for typing the manuscript, to Elizabeth Keyworth for her cheerful forbearance and to Charlotte and Christopher Keyworth for their occasionally welcome, but always refreshing interruptions. Finally we hope the others will forgive us if we suggest that the greatest debt is owed to our editor, Emma Myers, who has blessed us with efficiency, enthusiasm and good humour far beyond the call of duty.

1 The custom of giving notes

'I believe it [the Bank of England] is a very good fund, a very useful one, and a very profitable one. It has been useful to the Government, and it is profitable to the proprietors; and the establishing it at such a juncture, when our enemies were making great boasts of our poverty and want, was a particular glory to our nation and the City in particular'.[1]

Two years after its foundation in 1694, the Bank of England was described as 'one of the best establishments that ever was made for the good of the kingdom.'[2] Looking back over almost three hundred years, few would question that the Bank has become the Grand Old Lady not merely of Threadneedle Street but of all British banking. Throughout that time the policy of the Bank of England with regard to every aspect of banking has been relevant for all other banks in the country. Because of this position the Bank of England has been at different times copied, envied and condemned, but it has never been without influence. The design of Bank of England notes is therefore a point of reference to which the notes of other banks may be contrasted and compared. However, to understand the beginnings of British banking and to discover the earliest ancestor of our modern paper currency, we must look back beyond the foundation of the Bank of England, and even before the seventeenth century.

Early in the reign of Elizabeth I (1558–1603), the word 'banker' was used to refer to an exchange specialist.[3] Over the next century other people whose work involved handling valuables or money – merchants, brokers, scriveners and goldsmiths – began to act as financial agents. By the later seventeenth century the range of services available included loans, interest-bearing deposits, foreign coin exchange, cheques and notes.

The most common antecedent of the bank note seems to be the receipts which were given in exchange for deposits of cash. In the late sixteenth century money for loans to the Crown was raised by subscriptions in return for which Privy Seal notes were given, recording the lender's name, the amount lent, and a receipt. On the due date the lender was repaid at the Exchequer of Receipt and he endorsed the Privy Seal note with his signature. This procedure is strikingly similar to the first note issues of the Bank of England, whereby depositors received running cash notes as a receipt. These could then be redeemed in coin either to the full amount or in part, in which case the note would be endorsed and the outstanding sum noted.

The notes, receipts and cheques used by the earliest financial agents were

A request dated 1665, to pay £25-15s from an account held with Morriss and Clayton, scriveners in Cornhill. CM 1980—11—30—812. (214 × 141 mm)

simply hand-written documents and much paper money continued to be without any ornament or graphic design until well into the eighteenth century. This is because the notes were in effect direct personal contracts, the value and validity of which lay in the trust between banker and customer, and the fact that each was known (or at least reputed) to be financially sound. Even if a draft was endorsed and passed on to a third party, the same principle of trust applied. This system worked as long as banking was restricted to a very small circle. It was only as banking became formalised as a profession, a service to a wider public, that the need for distinctive note designs arose. Non-assignable notes, payable to bearer, could circulate throughout a whole community and be exchanged between strangers. Of course confidence in the note would still depend largely on the reputation of the bank, but the note itself had also to convey clearly its authority and value. Also, as the use of paper money increased, it was no longer practical to write each note out by hand. Printed forms, on which details such as date, serial number and signature could be entered by hand, could cope with the increased use and provide sufficient numbers, and carry some decorative engraved feature which would help to identify and fix the origin of the note in the public's mind.

The usefulness and desirability of the new bankers aroused much debate. Many people reserved their trust for gold and silver, seeing in paper an opportunity for sharp practice and the risk of credit inflation. A treatise on accountancy in 1636 simply dismissed bank accounts as 'needless here in England';[4] other critics went further and questioned the motives and probity

'The Custom of giving Notes hath so much prevailed amongst us that the Bank could hardly carry on Business without it.' Sir Theodore Janssen 'Discourse concerning Banks', 1697.
Pen and ink drawing on vellum showing an office in the Bank of England *c.*1695. Inscribed *M Laurens*.

of bankers. The disenchanted author of *The Mystery of the New Fashioned Goldsmiths or Bankers* condemned them for charging exorbitant interest rates on loans 'in a constant avowed breach of the Laws of the Kingdom' and 'contrary to the Laws of God.' He wondered why such people should be trusted, and asked 'whether any man that hath exercised the Mystery of Banking, hath living or dying, gone off the stage with a clear good Estate, all his Creditors being paid, fully paid.'[5] No doubt there was some truth in what he wrote, but modern capitalists can probably be more tolerant: this was, after all, private enterprise; naturally the goldsmith-bankers hoped for profits, and clearly many contemporaries thought this a fair price to pay for the services offered. The rich variety of banking schemes advanced throughout the seventeenth century bears witness to enthusiasm for the new profession. If individually many of these proposals were only dreams, and fantastic ones at that, together they suggest awareness of a commercial need, and the large numbers of goldsmith-bankers and other financial intermediaries show that customers did exist. One commentator, writing around the time the Bank of England was founded, described how 'All sorts of Paper creditt in Orders, Bills, Noats, Bonds, Assignments, etc., overflowed the Kingdom. All our wealth seem'd to consist in a little Gold and adulterated Silver; a world of wooden scores and paper sums.'[6] This particular writer in fact deplored such an expansion of credit but he provides evidence that many people were willing to do business on the strength of written promises and obligations. Uncertain as these transactions may have been, they paved the way towards an official and regular paper currency.

The Bank's Charter.
The Great Seal of
William and Mary was
appended on the
morning of 27 July
1694.

The Glorious Revolution of 1688 brought with it the political, religious and economic freedom which together created the climate in which Britain's rise to commercial and military pre-eminence in eighteenth-century Europe could take place. Amongst the many projects nurtured by this new-found freedom was one which was to have a profound effect on the economic and therefore the wider development of the nation. It was a concept which had been debated on and off for some forty-odd years[7] and which finally came to fruition in 1694, some six years after William of Orange came to the throne of England. That project was the Bank of England.

The decline in England's power and importance during the 100 years between the Armada and the Glorious Revolution has been mainly attributed to the political and economic chaos of that period. However, there was one ingredient which, even if there were blessed stability, was still essential for the nation's well-being and even independence. It was the well-spring that was, indirectly, to supply the financial power for the country's national and international trade and the source to which Government would turn in times of trouble for the capital it needed either to avert monetary crises, or to finance naval or military expenditure.

By the middle of the seventeenth century the more prescient projectors[8] were beginning to argue for some form of bank, often based on existing ones abroad; it was clear from the example of the Dutch that successful credit-based trading could benefit a nation in many ways and help to enlarge its sphere of influence. The political economist Sir William Petty had recognised this need when he wrote in 1682:

What Remedy is there if we have too little Money? We must erect a Bank, which well computed doth almost double the Effect of our coined Money; and we have in

The first meeting of the Court of Directors, the governing body of the Bank of England, took place in the afternoon of the day the Charter had been sealed.

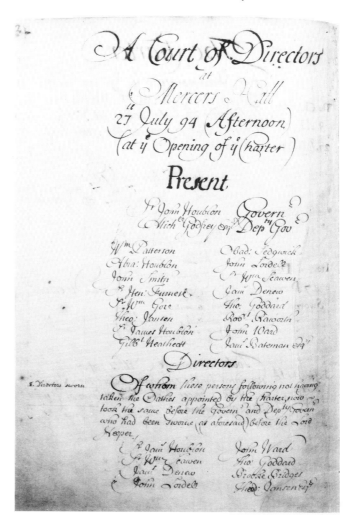

England Materials for a Bank which shall furnish Stock enough to drive the Trade of the whole Commercial World.[9]

Dutch William had brought to his adopted country an understandable desire to help his native country in its war against the French, and this proved to be the catalyst necessary for the idea of a national bank to be accepted, albeit grudgingly by some.

But it took a London-based Scots entrepreneur, William Paterson, to propose the scheme that eventually found favour: his first, proposed in 1691, had been rejected for several reasons. This was partly because, as he wrote in 1695, 'Others said this project came from Holland and therefore would not hear of it, since we had too many Dutch things already'.[10] But the interesting point about his initial scheme was that he and his backers required that in return for a loan of £1 million, the bills they issued should be made legal tender. This proved to be unacceptable to the Parliamentary Committee, and the scheme foundered, but after several more rejections Paterson put forward a plan[11] for a 'Bank of England' and a 'Fund for Perpetual Interest', although this time bills were not mentioned. Supported by two powerful personalities – Charles Montagu, Chancellor of the Exchequer, who looked after the

Sir John Houblon, first Governor of the Bank of England wearing mayoral robes. Grandson of a Huguenot refugee and companion of Samuel Pepys, he was an influential City merchant. From an oil painting by Isaac Whood.

The earliest known running cash note. Entirely hand-written. Dated 18 June 1697. (180 × 111 mm)

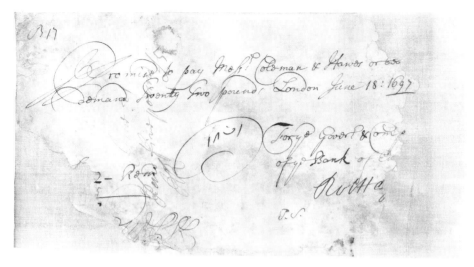

Parliamentary and Court lobbying, and Michael Godfrey, a leading merchant who ensured the idea's acceptance in the City – it was all but inevitable, given the Government's pressing need for funds, that the scheme should be approved by Parliament. Not surprisingly though, there was opposition from four groups: the Tories felt it would strengthen the position of the Whig Government and weaken theirs; the proto bankers – the goldsmiths, scriveners and money-lenders – saw the embryonic Bank as a powerful rival; others felt that the monarchy might become financially independent of Parliament; and some of the merchant fraternity believed it would become a too powerful trade rival carrying special privileges. The fears of the latter two groups were allayed in the drafting of the Bill: the Corporation was prohibited from lending to the Crown without Parliamentary consent and forbidden from engaging in trade. The Tories, on the other hand, were quite right to feel vulnerable: the promoters of the new Bank were Whigs to a man, indeed the historian Sir John Clapham described the Bank of the 1740s as being 'full of gold and Whiggery',[12] and the poor goldsmith-bankers, or as Paterson pejoratively spoke of them 'usurers and brokers of money',[13] were no longer to be at the centre of things financial. Previous Governments had gone to them when in need but at the end of the seventeenth century they did not have the scale of resources to respond adequately to such approaches; moreover their experiences of 1640 when Charles I seized depositors' cash housed in the Tower, and the 1672 Stop of the Exchequer when nearly £1 million was owed to the goldsmith-bankers had made them rather wary of officialdom. They preferred to do business on a much smaller scale with people they knew and could trust.

So Paterson's revised plan was accepted by Parliament; the Bank of England Act, 1694 (as it is always known nowadays) was passed; and arrangements were made for the taking-in of subscriptions which were to form the capital stock of the new project: the Bank of England. It was these subscriptions, totalling some £1.2 million, that were to be on-lent to Government in return for a Royal Charter, and subscribers were to receive a guaranteed income of eight per cent on their investment. This was Paterson's 'Fund for Perpetual Interest', which was, incidentally, the start of the funded National Debt described by Macaulay as 'that debt which has since become the greatest prodigy that ever perplexed the sagacity and confounded the pride of statesmen and philosophers'.[14]

Thus the money was raised, the Government paid, the Charter sealed and the Bank of England born. Paterson's successful proposal omitted to mention note issue as did the Charter, that orotund document which supposedly set out what the Bank as a corporate body could and could not do. It is unclear whether the omission was deliberate but it is clear that those who were

Sir Robert Clayton, the money-scrivener, in his mayoral robes. His country seat is shown in the background. He served as a Director of the Bank of England from 1702 until his death in 1707.
From an oil painting by Lorenzo da Castro.

A specie note for
£206-11s-10d dated
2 October 1697. In this
instance the depositor
George Martin paid in
'New money' – gold or
good silver coin – and
was entitled to be
repaid in the same.
(187 × 111 mm)

Detail from the
Specie note. It is the
earliest Britannia on an
issued note.

guiding and supporting the project were fully aware of the profitability of
issuing notes and intended to do so once the Bank had been established.
They were successful figures in the City, members of the new and burgeoning
middle class who had made their money through trade, but who looked
perhaps even a little enviously at established men of finance such as Robert
Clayton.[15] So it comes as no surprise that at their first meeting, a few hours
after the sealing of the Charter, the Directors of the Bank were discussing the
fundamental issue of 'the method of giving receipts for running cash'.[16]

Banking outside London

The foundation of the Bank of England in 1694 stands as a landmark for the
beginning of formal banking in Britain, but it was not until the second half of
the next century that banks emerged in any number throughout the country.
Compared with the highly-organised and inter-related banking network we

know today, these banks seem unstructured and unprofessional. Nevertheless, it was through their experiences, their successes and failures, that banking developed as a specialised business in its own right, in which note issue played a powerful supporting role.

Initially the number of banks in Britain grew slowly. The Bank of Scotland was set up in 1695, a year later than the Bank of England. The successful banking firm of Latouche in Ireland began as a combined poplin manufacturer and bank in 1693. Only two banks in the English provinces are known for the period before 1700.[17] The slow pace of growth continued in the new century; Edmund Burke's celebrated remark on a visit to England in 1750 that there were 'less than a dozen bankers' shops' is generally accepted as a reasonably accurate description of banking at that date. It is from the 1760s, in the early years of the Industrial Revolution, that banks and paper money promised to become significant elements in the workings of the British economy.

The chronology is not accidental. Banks were both a result and a cause of industrial expansion. In the English provinces, as in London, banking usually began as an expedient by-product of another business enterprise. Unlike in the capital, however, goldsmiths were not a particularly fertile ground for banking. Most often it was landowners, manufacturers and traders who offered banking services to meet local needs for payments and, via their London connections, the country-wide need for transfers of funds. The phenomenon conveniently labelled 'The Industrial Revolution' cannot be ascribed to any one cause. It was rather the result of a cross-fertilisation between ideas, various sources of wealth, and different industries, old and new. Country banks helped the seeds to take root by redistributing capital in two ways: locally, between businesses, and geographically, between agricultural areas with surplus funds and industrialising areas requiring financial investment. The growing industries needed both long- and short-term capital. Long-term fixed costs for raw materials and machinery were most likely to be met with credit arrangements, but short-term, variable costs − notably wages for an increasingly organised labour force, expecting regular payments − demanded a supply of ready cash. It was this short-term capital that country banks could provide, not least in the form of their own promissory notes. It is surely not coincidence that the textile and metal industries, both of which had a considerable need for variable capital investment, were two of the most prolific progenitors of early private banks. In the textile business we may mention Smiths of Nottingham, mercers with the distinction of opening the first known country bank; the Backhouses of Darlington, linen and worsted manufacturers who became very successful bankers; and the Mortlocks, woollen drapers in Cambridge. Samuel Alexander in Suffolk, and Lloyds in Birmingham, are two important examples of banks developing out of the iron industry.[18]

In Scotland banks began with a different emphasis but their livelihood was generally just as closely entwined with trade and industry. The major distinction between Scottish and English banks is that from the start private banking in Scotland had the clear identity of a specialised profession. The Bank of Scotland has been described as 'the first instance in Europe, and perhaps in the world, of a joint-stock bank formed by private persons for the express purpose of making a trade of banking, solely dependent upon private capital, and (apart from the legislation that created it) wholly unconnected with the state'.[19] Indeed, the Act of Incorporation expressly forbade the Bank from entering any other trade. The reference to joint-stock banking is important, for this was another characteristic which gave Scottish banks an advantage. By an Act of 1708 the Bank of England was given a monopoly of joint-stock banking in England; that is to say no other bank was allowed to have more than six partners. There was no such restriction in Scotland, and it is generally believed that this freedom encouraged the development of viable commercial banking on a scale to match economic growth. But while the Bank of Scotland was an independent corporate entity, legally and professionally, its founders and early directors were often merchants with experience of handling financial transactions. Furthermore, as its capital had no state backing, the Bank's success was dependent upon its customers' profitable involvement in agriculture, trade and industry. In this respect, then, the working capital for banks in Scotland, as in England, came from their connections with other lines of business. This similarity between the two banking systems is even more clearly seen in the beginnings of the Royal Bank of Scotland and the British Linen Company. The Royal Bank can be seen as a Scottish counterpart to the Bank of England: founded in 1727, it was a Whig enterprise, supported by Robert Walpole, the Prime Minister, and backed by the Equivalent fund; that is, the money paid by England to Scotland on the Union of 1707. The first directors of the Royal were predominantly lawyers and land-owners; they were, therefore, amateur bankers on a grand social scale like many of the founders of country banks in England. But, like its southern neighbours, the Royal Bank was actively concerned with promoting business. From its inception the Bank held £20,000 on interest-bearing deposit for the Board of Fisheries and Manufacturers; it also initiated a more flexible overdraft facility than the Bank of Scotland offered; and in the early 1730s it forged strong links with the dynamic Glasgow tobacco trade, which in turn provided the Royal with improved cash-flow and liquidity. Some years later, in 1749, merchants in the tobacco industry fostered the Ship Bank in Glasgow and gave it a good grounding, for it survived through various amalgamations to become part of the Union Bank in 1843. The British Linen Company owed its very existence to industry; it was founded under Royal Charter in 1746 primarily to promote linen manufacture in Scotland, but it was also explicitly permitted to bank.

Within a very few decades, banking replaced linen as the Company's main objective.

By the end of the eighteenth century the number of banks in Britain had risen from, almost literally, a handful of four or five at the end of the seventeenth, to several hundred. There may have been in the region of four hundred throughout England, the majority founded from the 1780s. Scotland had at least twenty-five banks, and several private note-issuers.

In consequence the amount of paper currency was also increasing dramatically. With the exception of notes offered in payment by the Bank of England, banker's notes were not legal tender; that is, there was no compulsion to accept them as payment of a debt. However, it appears that at least among the merchant class, bank notes were used quite readily. Lord Mansfield remarked in 1758 that bank notes were regarded 'as cash, in the ordinary course and transaction of business by the general consent of mankind, which gives them the credit and currency of money to all intents and purposes.' Indeed he said, 'They are as much money as guineas themselves are, or any other current coin that is used in common payment as money or cash.'[20]

Materials for a Bank

At their first meeting the Court of Directors considered the precise ways in which the Bank of England might conduct its business. At this stage they were more concerned with the deposit or cash aspect of the banking business rather than the management of Bank Stock; the remuneration for managing the latter had already been agreed and the mechanics of transfer and so on laid down in the Charter, so there was no call for this side of the Bank's business to be discussed. Deposit banking on the other hand, which included the issue of notes, must have seemed even more attractive, and when the Directors met for the first time – on the afternoon of Friday 27 July 1694, a few hours after the Charter had been sealed, a document which signally failed to limit the ambitions of the new Bank – they formalised three methods in which deposits would be acknowledged to customers.

Depositors would be permitted, the Court of Directors agreed, to choose one of three methods for having their deposits of cash – that is coin only – acknowledged; all three, incidentally, happened to be already practised by the goldsmith-bankers. The Bank would '. . . keep an Accompt with ye Creditor in a Book or Paper of his owne'; alternatively it might '. . . accept Notes drawn on ye Bank'; and finally it would '. . . give out Running-Cash-Notes and endorse on them what is paid off in part . . .'. The first method in principle is very similar to the way a modern building society account is operated today with a pass-book held by the customer; whilst in the second lies the origin of the cheque, for the customer received an 'acccomptable note' against which he could draw 'notes' (cheques) for himself or others on the

Bank. It is the third method which can justly lay claim to being the lineal forebear of the modern bank note; indeed it has been described by Sir John Clapham as the bank note *par excellence*.

Three days later the Directors appointed the first 'Servants of this House',[21] as Bank staff came to be known. Amongst the nineteen selected were three whose function was to authorise the receipts for running cash by signing them: they were John Kenrick (also written Kendrick) the First Cashier, at £200 per annum; Robert Hedges Second Cashier, at £100; and Thomas Maddocks (also written Madockes) Third Cashier, at £80; one of whose signatures completed the promissory clause on each note. Another crucial element in this compound was also decided upon that day. The Bank had been incorporated by Royal Charter, and as a corporation it needed a seal. Probably inspired by

The Bank of England appointed nineteen staff on 30 July 1694. From these appointments the three main departments of the Bank emerged: the Secretary's – legal, staff and domestic; the Accountant's – registrar of stocks; and the Cashier's – banking business including the issue of notes.

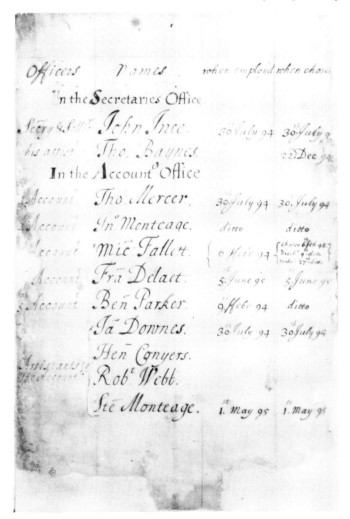

the fact that the Roettier-designed figure of Britannia had already been carried on halfpennies and farthings for some twenty years, the Directors minuted that the Bank's Common Seal should represent 'Britania sitting and looking on a Bank of mony [sic]'.[22] As a result of this decision Britannia was to appear on all printed Bank of England notes; indeed the Bank's Britannia, quite distinct from the Mint's for reasons which will be described later, has been put forward as a possible source for the Bank's nickname 'The Old Lady of Threadneedle Street'. As all printed Bank of England notes bore the Britannia vignette it is feasible that an inexpert engraver or an over-used copper plate might render her face less than regally. A glance at some of the earliest notes which display a distinct lack of consistency in the treatment of her facial characteristics confirms the plausibility of this theory, although it must be remembered that the Bank did not move its business to Threadneedle Street until 1734. Nevertheless it is just possible that 'The Old Lady' was a term used to describe the experiment which had by the middle of the eighteenth century turned into an institution.

As has already been mentioned the origins of the modern Bank of England note lie in the running cash note, one of the three issuing experiments initiated in the first few days of the Bank's existence; the Bank's running cash notes were, in their turn, modelled on those receipts issued by goldsmiths to their depositors. It was entirely logical that the Bank should choose to issue notes in a form that was familiar to the citizenry of London, for inextricably allied with familiarity is acceptability. The act of accepting a

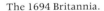
The 1694 Britannia.

A proof of a lettered
note engraved in 1694.
(207 × 111mm)

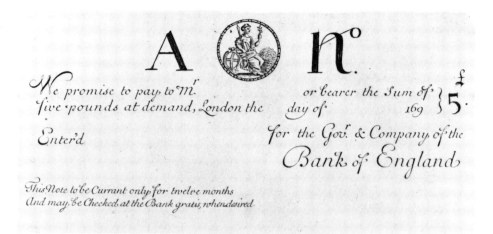

note is a mute testimony of trust in the issuer and faith in his promise to pay. This was not lost on the new breed of prudent and, at times, innovative bankers.

These receipts differed in one vital aspect from any other type in that they included after the name of the payee the words 'or Bearer' and it was this crucial ingredient which enabled them to circulate, albeit in a limited way. The Bank with its relatively large resources, Parliamentary backing and the acumen of its leadership was in a prime position to take over this branch of deposit banking and to develop and formalise it by partially printing the receipts which would be completed by hand at the time of issue: but there were to be problems. Although the Directors had decided four days after the Bank's legal genesis 'that the Running Cash Notes be printed' and copper plates engraved for five denominations (£5, £10, £20, £50 and £100), it seems almost certain that they were never issued then. The reason is recorded in the Court Minute Book: 'The Notes for Running Cash being considered liable to be counterfeited, for preventing thereof it was ordered that they be done on marbled paper Indented'.[23] In the meantime notes would have had to have been handwritten although no examples have survived.

However the new issue took some time to come to fruition and the order for printing was not given until the summer of 1695. No sooner had the new notes been issued than a forgery was discovered.[24] The reaction was swift and predictable: all running cash notes were to be handwritten; but an investigation was commissioned[25] into the feasibility of using specially water-marked paper. This eventually bore fruit in the summer of 1697 when the papermaker Rice Watkins produced at his mill in Sutton Courtenay, Berkshire, paper with a distinctive watermark; it had a looped border with scroll on the left and a panel with 'Bank of England' at the bottom.[26] A key security measure was thus introduced to Bank of England notes.

Yet despite the obvious advantages of paper money it had its detractors: the author of a pamphlet published in 1695 accused the Bank of acting illegally in connection with the note issue. He wrote:

they give their Cashires' [sic] Notes for all sums (ad infinitum) which neither charge the Fund [the original capital of £1.2 million] nor the Proprietors [the Stockholders], which seems to be a credit beyond the intention of the Act of Parliament, and never practiced [sic] before by any Corporation, to give Notes but under their Seal; and is almost a Fraud on the Subject.[27]

Perhaps the anonymous pamphleteer had been irked by the Bank paying the final instalment of the £1.2 million loan, a sum in excess of £44,000, in running cash notes. But it had been paid over to the Exchequer itself (well within the deadline of 1 January 1695, incidentally) and in the new medium to boot. As Sir John Clapham succinctly put it, 'The circulating note functions'.[28]

We now come to consider the information which the promissory note had to carry and the impact it had on the countenance of the note. It was a promissory note because the Bank undertook to pay, or perhaps more accurately, repay, to the depositor or the bearer the amount of his deposit whenever requested to do so. Although nowadays we have notes representing units of value rather than deposits of cash, most of the constituent parts of those early notes have, surprisingly, survived and are present in today's notes.

Those early partially-printed notes bear the Bank's common seal, are dated and numbered, and promise to pay 'A' or Bearer a sum of money which is written in words and figures. The undertaking to pay is signed on behalf of the Bank by one of its cashiers. Today's notes similarly carry the Bank's seal, are numbered but not dated (the last date to appear on a note was 1956), have a shortened promissory clause to 'Bearer' only, the amount in words and figures, and the printed signature of the Chief Cashier.

Two Britannias from 1703 notes. Clearly the work of different engravers. Note the two styles of treatment of the shading.

Three supposedly identical Britannias taken from unissued lettered notes. Differences in the facial features, hair and pile of money are particularly noticeable.

The common seal of the Bank was (and still is), of course, Britannia. The Bank Britannia differs from the one favoured by the Mint in one important aspect: whereas the Mint's has a decidedly nautical flavour – she carries a trident and often the sea forms the backcloth – the Bank's is definitely land-based. She holds a spear in one hand and an olive branch in the other and looks on the 'Bank of mony'. The characteristics of that first Britannia are well-documented and there are many extant examples on the covers of the earliest books of account depicting her as a well-endowed post-Restoration beauty in flamboyant pose. From there the Britannia vignette developed with successive designer-engravers – several different versions appeared within the first few years – and soon the 'Bank of mony' began to resemble a skep, the plaited straw beehive, and later still a flight-hole is clearly apparent. The olive branch developed into the English plant honesty. The frame of the vignette moved from a series of dots, to a circle of stars and then on to foliations which were endowed with a crown in 1732. These two features – crown and foliations – were to remain for well over two hundred years until 1961 when the 1855 Maclise-designed Britannia was discarded with the withdrawal of the 1928-style ten shilling note. The presence of Britannia has been a convenient vehicle for yet another anti-forgery device. Certainly in the nineteenth century the sophistication of the Maclise design was intended to discourage forgery. Similarly the dating and numbering of notes, originally by hand and merely recording the ledger entry, eventually became points on which the forger could be tripped up. The promissory clause is short and to the point: 'I promise to pay to . . . or Bearer on demand the summe of . . . London the . . . day of . . . For the Govr and Comp^a of the Bank of England.' There are two interesting points here: firstly that the singular 'I' should have been used; for, whilst it is true that the document was signed by one person, it is also indisputable that the phrase 'Governor and Company' is plural. (Curiously the 1694 denominational notes which were printed but never issued used the plural.) The second point concerns the typeface chosen because it was not, as might have been expected, a bold plain forme, but one

A partly-printed running cash note of 1699 for £62-15s-0d signed by Thomas Madockes. Initially it was partially encashed leaving a balance of £8-1s-11d. (200 × 113 mm)

which echoed the cursive script of the goldsmiths' handwritten notes: evidence of the aim to retain familiarity of design perhaps?

Throughout the eighteenth century the issue of notes by the Bank grew apace aided on occasion by legislation; but whilst the uses which the notes themselves represented grew more sophisticated the methods by which they were produced certainly did not, nor did the overall design of the notes to any significant degree. Printing was still carried out using the time-honoured method of engraved copper plates. Alterations tended to be piecemeal and small. On the one hand it could be argued that the design was unimaginative and begging the question of a response to the problems of forgery, and on the other that the 'familiarity' argument dictated a policy of variations upon the theme, even though it was a theme which had been established before the turn of the century. Whatever the reasons, the policy, or perhaps lack of it, was to ensure that a radical re-think of the design of the Bank's notes did not occur until the rampant forgery of the Restriction period (1797–1821) when the public outcry at the number of capital convictions for this offence compelled the Bank to conduct a crusade for a supposedly inimitable note. But the only tangible outcome of these investigations was that the Bank adopted a waved line watermark for its notes. Eventually a new note – but only new by dint of the technological advances used to produce it – came out in 1855. Predictably it was almost indistinguishable from its predecessors.

But while printing methods hardly altered in the eighteenth century, bank note paper improved. In 1724, Henry Portal, a Huguenot refugee, was contracted to make and deliver to the Governor and Company '. . . Paper for Bank Notes of the like Goodness or fitter for their Service than the paper now used . . .'.[29] The Bank had probably been spurred on to this action by the criticism of a condemned forger, George Nicholas, who had proved very cooperative when

Detail from a 1757 £90 note. The Sum block or Sum piece, an elaborate £ sign followed by the amount in white Gothic letters on a black ground, was introduced in 1743.

visited in Newgate in 1722 by a Bank Cashier, Wollaston Shenton. Nicholas had altered the amount of a note from £11 to £80. The paper was spongy and brown, the forger had said, if it had been harder and whiter he would not have been able to erase the amount by using chemicals. Also he volunteered that if the amount of a note should '. . . appear on the reverse of the Note in figures against the figures on the front' then erasure would not be feasible;[30] it was an idea that was to surface again almost a century later.

The first denominationalised notes were printed in 1725 on the new Portals paper which was of better quality than the one it replaced. The watermark was unchanged other than that the words 'Bank of England' were now in Roman rather than *Italic* script. The new notes, still partially printed, were for round amounts although they could be written up on issue by the Bank to the amount required by the customer, thus a £20 note could be amended to read £29–19–11.

A further change (still not a substantial one) occurred in 1743 with the arrival of the 'Sum Block', an elaborate £ sign followed by the amount in white Gothic letters on a black ground. The black bead-like projections to the border of the background gradually became more defined and each denomination had its own particular pattern. Essentially it was a device to prevent erasure and subsequent alteration of the amount.

The administrative machinery was now in place to ensure the supply of notes, and the public were becoming increasingly content to accept these paper promises for purely pragmatic reasons. For example if a note were lost the Bank would issue another, admittedly under indemnity; also a 'stop' could be placed against a note if, say, it had been stolen. The accidental loss of a small piece of a note would not necessarily invalidate it or affect its face-value but the same could hardly be said for the coinage. In fact at times when the coinage was in a particularly parlous state notes were often preferred by the public in order to avoid the risk of having to handle coins whose value had been diminished by clipping or filing.

Establishing an identity

Insofar as country banks were often the result of developing industry, their promissory notes were also a response to the shortage of coin and short-term credit at a time when demands for capital were increasing. However, the notes had a dual nature, for they were to some extent a self-perpetuating phenomenon, generating business for the banks. Issuing their own notes was an important way of making banks known within a community and of attracting custom. Walter Bagehot, constitutional historian and banker, explained how a banker might begin business with very little capital, and use note issue to bring in deposits:

In what form the best paper currency can be supplied to a country is a question of economical theory with which I do not meddle here. I am only narrating unquestionable history, not dealing with an argument where every step is disputed. And part of this certain history is that the best way to diffuse banking in a community is to allow the banker to issue bank notes of small amount that can supersede the metal currency.[31]

Bagehot argued that as people accumulated many notes from one banker, they would in time realise that they were already placing so much trust in the bank that they might as well deposit money there for safe-keeping. But this process depended on the publicity provided by the notes, and on the extent of banking within a country, thus:

The credit of the banker having been efficiently advertized by the note, and accepted by the public, he lives on the credit so gained years after the note issue itself has ceased to be very important to him. The efficiency of this introduction is proportional to the diffusion of the right of note issue. A single monopolist issuer, like the Bank of France, works its way with difficulty through a country, and advertizes banking very slowly.[32]

On the other hand local bankers could advertise banking and attract deposits because they knew and were known by local people. The best note issue to advance the business of banking was 'one made by individuals resident in the district, and conversant with it.'[33] Britain provided an excellent case in point: 'In England and Scotland a diffused system of note issues started banks all over the country . . .'[34] Indeed, Bagehot claimed it was to money deposited with these banks and then sent to the capital, that London owed her status as one of the world's great money markets.

How then did bankers of the eighteenth century advertise themselves on their notes? The appearance of the notes was essentially the format that had been established by the Bank of England with its very first issues of 1694. Notes were printed from engraved copper plates, in black ink on white paper. They were rectangular in shape, with the exception of many Scottish notes which were often square. The wording of the notes usually followed the formula 'I/We promise to pay X or Bearer on demand the sum of _____ value received.' The place of issue was generally printed, but the date and serial number were filled in by hand, and all notes were hand-signed. Many notes were plain and unadorned, sometimes with no decoration beyond the printed text. However even some of the plainer designs incorporated ideas which foreshadowed anti-forgery devices used in the nineteenth and twentieth centuries.

The lettering itself offered opportunities for early security printing. The text of the note was usually in copperplate script, but a different type was likely to be used for the denomination, the name of the bank, or the town of issue. One or other of these three subjects generally appeared at the top centre of the note, often with an elaborate initial letter erupting into a series of flourishes flowing round the whole word. Frequently these graceful flourishes were echoed in elegant scroll patterns forming a counterfoil down the left-hand side of the note. Issued notes would have an indented edge cut through the design, so that the two pieces could be matched for identification. These scroll-work counterfoils are one of the most common features on eighteenth-

A cheque dated 1767 with an elaborate scroll counterfoil, drawn on an account held with the London bankers Boldero, Carter, Barnston & Snaith.
CM 1980–11–30–719.
(205 × 79 mm)

29

century notes; sometimes the name of the bank or the initials of the partners' names were worked into the pattern. Notes issued by the Bank of Scotland from the 1720s to the 1780s show clearly the variations possible with just these two security devices. Printing individual words or letters in a different typeface was intended to prevent alterations of the denomination, and to aid detection of forgeries. Successive issues of the one pound note carried changing and increasingly complicated designs of scroll-work, and several very different styles of alphabet, ranging from cursive round hand and regal Old English to spiky court hand, were used within the text.

This was the basic formula for eighteenth-century note design, and many banks' notes had no more decoration than the scroll and lettering. Others, however, adopted another device used by the Bank of England from its early days, and included a small engraved vignette, or other ornamental cipher, usually in the top left-hand corner of the note. The devices were an opportunity both to discourage forgery, and to give the bank and its notes a distinctive identity. Probably the most common subject was a monogram of the initials of the partners' names or the name of the bank, but almost as popular was a local coat of arms. Also seen, but less frequently in this period than later, were views or emblems of local interest – for example, a sailing ship at sea on notes of the Southampton Commercial Bank – and allegorical figures, such as

A Bank of Scotland note for £12 Scots (£1 sterling) of 1723, incorporating several different typefaces. The denomination is printed in words to discourage alteration. CM 1983–11–9–19. (120 × 136 mm)

An 18th-century unissued note from the Sheffield Bank is decorated with a floral monogram of the partners' initials. CM 1981—11—22—566. (188 × 76 mm)

Even private issues for small change might carry some ornamentation. This 5s note of 1788 signed by David Wright of Wainfleet has a border of stylised leaves. CM PM—416. (79 × 54 mm)

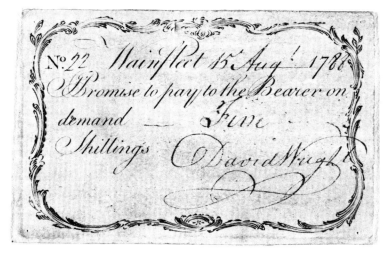

This sheep from a 10 guinea note of the Shepton Mallet and Somersetshire Bank is an unusual vignette for an eighteenth century note. (detail). CM 1981—11—22—571. 200 × 96 mm)

(Far left) Monogram on shield surrounded by a looped flower garland, engraved by Ashby for a 5 guinea note of the Manchester New Bank, 1791. (detail) CM 1986–10–31–63 190 × 97 mm)

(Left) Lions and herrings on the coat of arms of Great Yarmouth, framed with olive branches, on a 5 guinea note of the Great Yarmouth Bank, 1783. (detail) CM 1980–11–30–159. 182 × 108 mm)

Britannia or Pallas. The engraving was sometimes elegant, sometimes crude; almost always simple. It is perhaps appropriate that an attractive and unusual exception is a detailed city view of Nottingham, appearing on a note of 1746 from Abel Smith & Co., the earliest recorded provincial banker. There seems little doubt that individual designs could make an impact on the public: three private banking partnerships begun in Glasgow in the middle of the century became known colloquially by names drawn from their vignettes; thus, the Ship Bank, the Thistle Bank, and the Glasgow Arms Bank.

Looking back at eighteenth-century notes, the predominant characteristic is the lack of ornament, the austerity of design. Indeed, the simplicity and formality of these notes (themselves drawing on an earlier heritage) established traditional features which persisted into the nineteenth century and later. Nevertheless there were instances of experimental and adventurous note designs, daring for their time, but forerunners of future developments. An outstanding innovation was the use of colour. Colour on notes was not generally adopted in Britain until well into the nineteenth century, but it was first used much earlier. As early as the 1760s a London banking partnership, Boldero, Carter, Barnston and Snaith, used brightly-coloured marbled paper for the counterfoil on the left-hand end of their cheques. The honour of first printing in colour on circulating notes is accorded to the Royal Bank of Scotland, which introduced an unusual guinea note in 1777. Printed as usual with black type on white paper, with a scroll at the left-hand edge, the note also carried the words 'One Guinea' in white on a blue panel at the top right-hand corner, and, to the left, a profile portrait of George III as he appeared on the guinea coin, printed in red. It is interesting, though, that the role of calligraphy was not up-staged by this innovation; the text boasts at least half a dozen distinct lettering styles.

Early use of a
panoramic city view
on a £20 note dated
1746 from Smith's of
Nottingham, the first
English provincial
bank. (detail)
*By courtesy of the
National Westminster
Bank.*

In other respects than design, eighteenth-century bank notes gave hints of things to come. The forgery of notes, faced by the Bank of England within a few days of the first issue, became a recurring problem for banks throughout the country. In the long term, many improvements in the production and design of notes were motivated by the need to keep one step ahead of the forgers. For the time being, however, emphasis was laid more on cure than prevention.

Of great encouragement to the counterfeiter was the low level of literacy prevailing in Britain. Exact figures are notoriously hard to determine, but one may fairly safely assume that about half the population could neither read nor write in the middle of the eighteenth century. A large number of people were therefore ill-equipped to judge the authenticity or otherwise of money consisting mainly of written words. In fact, the forgers' opportunity arose partly from the paradoxical dual nature of bank notes: as a general form of money they were familiar enough for people to accept them, but the notes of any particular bank were obviously not always well enough known for a forgery to be immediately detected. This dual personality is apparent in the phenomenon of bogus or skit notes, which proliferated in the late eighteenth and early nineteenth centuries. These notes were generally intended as a joke, used as a form of advertising, or for calling attention to a public issue, and their appearance, copying bank notes, suggests that the public were sufficiently familiar with notes to see the visual pun. They were not intended as a criminal fraud, but were sometimes used to deceive the unwary.

The 'Scale-de-Cross' Bank near Newcastle provides a good example. Notes bearing this completely bogus name were issued in the 1780s, copying the notes of the new Commercial Bank in Newcastle. At first glance they look plausibly like a country bank five pound note, but on closer examination they turn out to be worth only five ha'pence. It is possible that they were printed to be sold for charity, but at least one person thought differently. In 1787 at a fair in Newcastle, Hugh Peel, a horse-dealer, gave a Scale-de-Cross note in payment of five pounds for a mare 'to an unlettered person.' He was convicted of fraudulent deceit, and sentenced to twelve months imprisonment.[35]

The problem of distinguishing between real and spurious notes was even more acute when the bank in question really existed. In November 1765 a Scottish paper carried an advertisement from a gentleman who had 'presented eight or ten British Linen Company twenty shillings notes for payment at their office, one whereof they alledged to be forged; which may be true, although, from comparison with those they call their own notes, with much difficulty the difference can be discerned, the forged note is so like a real one. . . .' A postscript from an official of the British Linen Company explained that the offending item had been inscribed by the teller with the words '*A forged note*', so that no-one else would be taken in.[36]

As we have seen, some banks did introduce more complex note designs to dissuade forgers, but for the most part, they seem to have relied on punishment as a deterrent. When in 1785, two years after it was set up, the Court of the Bank of Ireland decided to prosecute in all cases of forgery,[37] they were following a well-established precedent. In 1765 a Newcastle forger was sentenced to transportation, having been convicted by the damaging evidence of his mistress, and the beleaguered British Linen Company went to considerable expense in prosecuting a Dundee schoolmaster who had forged their notes, amongst others, the previous year. Two pocket-books were found in his bed-clothes, containing 'seven pieces of paper cut to the dimensions of the British Linen Company, and smoked, or otherwise discoloured, to a resemblance of the paper of that company's notes after being some time in circulation'.[38] After a difficult trial, in which the defence tried, unsuccessfully, to claim that the British Linen Company's notes were not a legally binding promise of payment, and therefore could not be criminally forged, the defendant was sentenced to be placed in the pillory in Edinburgh, wearing a label saying '*Infamous Forger*' and then 'to be transported to America, never to return to Scotland.'[39]

In the following century, while punishment for forgery remained severe, greater efforts were made to prevent the crime by rendering notes more difficult of imitation. That relatively little was done in this direction in the eighteenth century can be explained, at least in part, by current trends in engraving and printing.

Design and society

Just as bankers were a product of industrial development, so their notes bear witness to the artistic tastes and printing techniques of their time. The early flowering of banking as a profession in the later eighteenth century was part of a new phase of economic growth, which brought new opportunities for displaying wealth and social status. With the emergence of a new middle-class eager for culture, the potential for a mutually beneficial relationship between art and commerce became more and more apparent. The union was fruitful, giving birth to neo-classical design on a grand scale for public architecture, and more intimately to Adam interiors for private homes, Wedgwood pottery for the new decor, and stately homes and museums to whet the public appetite. As good taste became a prerequisite for social rank, art and design became marketable products. Their popularity and importance was reflected in a flurry of specialist societies and art schools: the Society of Artists (1755), the Trustees Academy in Edinburgh (1760), the Royal Academy (1768) and the Society for the Encouragement of Arts, Manufactures and Commerce (1754) which proclaimed by its very name the affinity between these three. Many of these bodies were investments in the art of the future; they awarded prizes for drawing and design to young people, and the full impact of their training was in many cases not apparent until the early nineteenth century. However, their beginnings are proof of the tremendous surge of interest in the fine arts in the second half of the eighteenth century.

Closely allied to this expansion of commerce and art was the development of printing and engraving. Improved communications and the growth of trade generated an increasing need for printed business correspondence, which might previously have been practicably executed by hand: bank notes and other negotiable instruments are obvious examples. Socially, the growing interest in public issues, literature and the fine arts stimulated the reproduction of illustrated tracts and books, and prints of engravings from paintings. There was, however, a difference in social emphasis and effect between the rise of interest in fine arts, and the growth in output of printing. Whereas the fine arts of painting, sculpture and architecture produced splendid works which conferred a certain cachet on both the artist and the customer, printing and engraving remained the prerogative of numerous small-scale businesses producing a wide range of less exotic items for daily life such as trade cards, advertising posters, theatre bills, bottle-labels, newspapers, political handbills, legal documents and chapbooks. Many of their products are categorised now as ephemera, but they should be spared the unfair connotation of triviality: like so many ordinary aspects of our past, their importance is easily overlooked. Most printers worked in London, but towards the end of the eighteenth century, an increasing number could be found in the burgeoning provincial towns, disseminating basic information on local trade, politics, education and entertainment. The contribution made by printers to a changing economy and society was therefore considerable, but as far as history is concerned, it is often anonymous.

Clearly the business of most printers depended on their versatility, and note-issuing banks must have been a useful new source of employment. The two main forms of printing in the eighteenth century were relief printing, such as letterpress, and intaglio, such as copper-engraving or etching. The

The Bank's name
embellished with
decorative flourishes,
on an 18th-century
5 guinea note of the
Shrewsbury Bank.
CM 1981–11–82–576.
(212 × 93 mm)

art of copper-engraving, dating back to the fifteenth century, was traditionally associated with pictorial illustration and decorative texts, and so it was well suited to the production of bank notes, which used precisely these forms of ornament. Two aspects in particular stand out. Firstly, the emphasis on beautifully-formed lettering for the text of notes drew on a late seventeenth-century legacy of fine calligraphy. A modern writer, introducing a twentieth-century edition of George Bickham's *The Universal Penman*, first published in the 1740s, attributes this new art form to the growth of commerce, requiring 'a round, even flowing hand for business correspondence.'[40] Bickham himself admitted that there were already 'a large variety of Copy-Books, and several of them executed by able and very accurate Penmen',[41] but he confidently explained that: 'The Use of the Pen is of so great Importance to Mankind in general, and so indispensably necessary for the Man of Business, that I think it needless to make any Apology for the Publication of this Work.'[42] Among Bickham's specimens of fine writing were fictitious examples of letters of credit, bills of exchange, and 'Banker's Notes', all plausibly reproducing the form and fluid running script of both hand-written and printed early notes. Their elegance and restraint demonstrated, too, Bickham's recommendation of 'Plain, Strong and neat Writing . . . to which may be added such ornamental Turns of the Pen, as seem rather design'd to fill up Vacancies on the Paper, than studiously compos'd to adorn the Piece.' He warned against excessive decoration for, 'In Flourishing the Fancy would be so Luxuriant, was it not corrected by the Judgement, as almost to destroy the End of Writing; as Airs in Musick, when too often repeated, or too long or too variously performed, disorder the Harmony of a just Composure.'[43] That eighteenth-century bank note design did not on the whole commit this error is probably due to a combination of good taste and practical limitations; the fussy security printing on some nineteenth-century notes suggests that the engravers were simply carried away by the more advanced printing techniques available.

The other element in contemporary art which found a place on bank notes was the vignette, or small-scale engraving, which was particularly encouraged by the popularity of illustrated books. At their best these engravings were gorgeous: mezzotints, stipple-engravings, colour etchings, and caricatures allowed a marvellous range of expression, from rich allegory to punchy humour. But it must be said that as far as bank notes are concerned, the pictorial vignettes often did not live up to the quality of the calligraphy. An early twentieth-century writer suggests that 'In the eighteenth century, printing gave little encouragement to engravers, hence they were few, their work was dear, and often poor in result. This kept the banks from expending money upon an elaborate design and simplified the work of the forger.'[44]

Whether engravers were really so short of work is questionable, but it may well be the case that bankers with still limited note circulation were unwilling to pay for top-quality work. This must have been particularly true of the many unofficial issuers of small notes for under one pound; for example, an English note from Wainfleet for five shillings, just a square of card with a slim garland border, or a note for three Scottish pounds from Dunkeld, with a bird in a circlet. Moreover it seems to have been usual for provincial bankers to turn to local printers and engravers, and these were generally small businesses – perhaps only a master and his assistant. They too were unlikely to have had enough capital to experiment with the newest or most sophisticated methods of reproduction, and it must be remembered that, although engraving was increasing in popularity, it still had a low profile in comparison with other branches of the arts. Official institutions were not supportive; for example, in its first year, only four of the Royal Academy's seventy-seven students studied engraving.[45] It was a question of snobbery, and of knowing your market. As Hogarth realised, fine painting earned social respectability, while prints could spread a message and make your name among a wider range of classes. But for the latter, 'Neither minute accuracy of design, nor fine engraving was deemed necessary, as the latter would render them too expensive for the persons for whom they were intended to be useful.'[46] If that was Hogarth's experience, how much less incentive must there have been for the numerous, unknown provincial engravers, working for limited local markets?

The appearance of eighteenth-century notes was dictated – we might say limited – by the uncertainty within the relatively new profession of banking itself, by contemporary aesthetic values, and by the available and affordable methods of printing. But it would be unfair to stress only their shortcomings. The notes were products of their age; they were part of a revolution in industry and society, and were themselves a revolutionary new form of general currency. In the closing years of the century the demands of these changes combined with war to place extraordinary pressures on the young banking system, and to challenge the traditional design of its notes.

2 A crisis of confidence

'an elderly lady in the City, of great credit and long standing who had . . . unfortunately fallen into bad company.'[1]

'. . . the issue of Notes for very small amounts is a great incentive to forgery.'[2]

The Bank and William Pitt

When on the morning of Monday 27 February 1797 members of the public who came to the Bank's offices in Threadneedle Street to change their notes for cash could not do so, it was because an instruction had been issued to the Bank by the Privy Council[3] at the instigation of the Prime Minister, William Pitt.[4] For the first time Bank of England notes were declared inconvertible, and they were to remain so for some twenty-four years until cash payments were resumed on 15 May 1821. During that time, commonly known as the Restriction Period, much criticism was aimed at the Bank's Directorate because of their seemingly unimaginative and intransigent attitude towards changes in note design and the poor quality of the printing which certainly did nothing to deter forgery, particularly of the newly-issued one and two pound notes. As the forgery of bank notes was a capital offence, the Bank's Directorate acquired an unenviable, and largely undeserved, reputation of, as the *Black Dwarf*, a contemporary journal, put it, 'grand purveyors to the gibbet'.[5]

The events leading to the imposition of the Restriction had begun some twenty years before with the drain of gold to America during the War of Independence; and when William Pitt the Younger became Prime Minister in 1783 his demands on the Bank and perpetual search for funds to finance government expenditure continued to place pressure on the Bank's reserves – part of which of course backed the note issue. In 1790, still looking for unemployed funds, he had proposed, much to the dismay of the Bank, to requisition unclaimed dividends on the Public Funds.[6] A compromise was eventually reached but so began a sometimes stormy relationship between Premier and national (but still privately-owned) bank that lasted throughout his term of office. It was this relationship between Pitt and the Bank, capped by his stoppage of cash payments, that led to Sheridan's description of the latter as 'an elderly lady in the City, of great credit and long standing who had . . . unfortunately fallen into bad company'.[7] This provided the raw material for James Gillray's cartoon in which the Bank is depicted as an old lady wearing a dress of the newly-issued one pound notes and seated on a strongbox of gold, seemingly being wooed by Pitt who, ignoring the paper money, is only interested in gold. Entitled 'Political Ravishment or The Old Lady of Threadneedle Street in danger' it is the earliest known instance of the Bank's nickname appearing in print. Pitt's epitaph in the context of bank notes was rather unkindly and anonymously penned thus:

> Of Augustus and Rome the poets still warble
> How he found it of brick and left it of marble,
> So of Pitt and England men say without vapour
> How he found it of gold and left it of paper.

Yet another move towards the inevitable 'Restriction' came in 1793 when the Revolutionary Government of France declared war on England. This

The Bank informed the public of the stoppage of cash payments by means of this notice published on 27 February 1797.

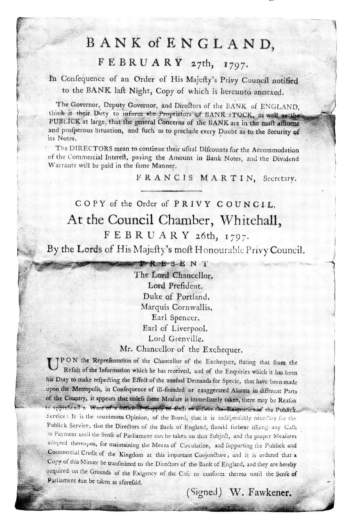

'Murder! murder! Rape! murder!
O you Villain! what have I kept my Honor
untainted so long, to have it broke up, by you at last?
O Murder! Rape! Ravishment! Ruin! Ruin, Ruin!!!

POLITICAL-RAVISHMENT,—or,—The Old Lady of Threadneedle-Street in danger!

'Political Ravishment; or the Old Lady of Threadneedle Street in Danger.' The Bank, represented by an old lady, whose dress is made of the newly-issued £1 and £2 notes, is being wooed by a rapacious William Pitt the Younger, who ignores the paper money and goes for gold in her pocket and treasure chest.
By James Gillray. Published 22 May 1797.
(354 × 247 mm)

served only to exacerbate the commercial crisis which had begun in the previous autumn and now threatened to bring the nation's industry to a standstill. The Bank's answer to the run on itself was the traditional one: restrict the note issue and raise the discount rate. But as the weakest banking houses started to go to the wall pressure mounted on the remainder, who, in order to stay solvent, refused to discount altogether and locked away their cash.[8] Clearly something had to be done to prevent the ultimate stagnation of production; consequently on 2 April 1793 the Court Minute Book recorded that 'With the present situation of Credit and the want of confidence in many of the Country Bankers it is expedient for the present Emergency that Five pound Bank Notes be issued by the Bank of England . . .'. The new issue was announced in the *London Gazette* on 16 April and the notes were available at the Bank two days later.

This increase in the circulation – the Bank's total issue later that year stood at £12.2 million,[9] higher than it had ever been before – seems to have been the answer for by the middle of the following year the bullion reserves had increased along with confidence generally. However it was to be short-lived because of the flow of bullion to Europe once France had given up her unsuccessful attempt to convert her populace to paper money. At the same time of course there were the by now familiar continual demands on the Bank's reserves by Pitt, leading to repeated warnings from the Bank that he should not rely on further help.

Pitt was determined, not unreasonably, to ensure that if necessary he would leave no stone unturned in his search for funds when the very survival of the country was at stake; whilst the Bank, which on the one hand had already slipped quite naturally into the role of the national bank, on the other, still had an obligation towards its stockholders. It had, somehow, to strike a balance between Pitt's demands, the interests of its stockholders and the welfare of the nation. Of course Pitt's aims were not incompatible with the Bank's and, although it may have complained sometimes at his insatiability, whenever it could comply, it did.

The threat of an invasion towards the end of 1796 caused some withdrawal and hoarding of gold, and the report in February the following year of a landing by French troops in Wales caused enough alarm to spur Pitt into protecting the Bank's reserves against panic withdrawals. For some time he had been kept informed by deputations from the Bank pointing out the gradual depletion of the cash reserves – on 21 February the Bank's stock of coin stood at not much more than £1 million and £90,000 had been withdrawn on 23 February and £130,000 on the following day; his response had been to offer 'to bring forward in the [Privy] Council for a proclamation to stop the issue of cash from the Bank and to give the Security of Parliament to the Notes of the Bank'. News of the Welsh landing arrived in London on 25 February and although as it turned out it only consisted of a few hundred men led by an Irish-American adventurer and was easily put down, the damage had been done. It was now time for action: seeing that his supply of gold at the Bank was threatened Pitt called a meeting of the Privy Council and the Directors were ordered not to pay cash for notes until Parliament had considered the matter.

First appearing in 1793, the £5 note is the longest continuously-serving denomination. (195 × 120 mm)

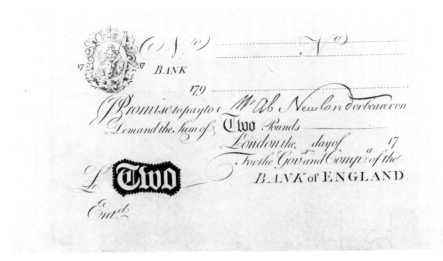

An unissued 1797 £2 note. The 1797 £1 note also followed this pattern. For legal reasons notes at this time could not be made payable simply to bearer and so the Bank chose to insert the name of the Chief Cashier, Abraham Newland, in the payee clause.
(202 × 120 mm)

The result was predictable: the limitation on the supply of gold and silver coin inevitably pushed bullion prices higher and so people clung to their cash. In this respect the situation four years before, when the Bank had brought out a new and lower denomination note (the five pound note), was not dissimilar, and nor was the remedy this time. The Bank began issuing one and two pound notes to take the place of guineas which could no longer be obtained; but no-one could have foreseen the price in terms of human suffering that would have to be paid because of this public-spirited gesture.

The new notes tended to be handled by a section of the population unused to paper money; often illiterate, they found it difficult if not impossible to tell the genuineness of the new notes. With coins it was a different matter. It was naturally easy to identify gold and silver when one had been used to handling coins since childhood, and literacy was not a prerequisite for using a balance and a coin known to be of the correct weight. So the stage was set for an outbreak of forgery and these people became the natural dupes of the forger and his accomplices. To make matters worse the new hastily-prepared notes were a poor piece of work;[10] old worn-out plates used for higher denominations had been re-engraved and the result was not the printers' best. The new notes were the same size as other denominations, and layout and style followed the same pattern. This was changed in the following year when a new, clearer, perhaps even slightly distinctive, design was introduced because, as was minuted in January 1798,[11] of 'the designs of evil-intentioned persons who are endeavouring to impose on the Public by putting off forged notes as the small notes of the Bank of England'. The printed area was reduced and enclosed by a line, and at the centre top the denomination appeared in letters; but again this was a short-lived issue.

Reverting to using the whole note for the printing and continuing the

Extensive forgery of the new low-denomination notes caused the design of them to be revised a year later. £1 note dated 13 July 1798. (200 × 113 mm)

search for inimitability, the Bank looked towards the paper of its notes for the key, as indeed it had done when forgery threatened in the very first months of its existence. This time a new and distinctive waved line watermark was introduced that ultimately became the hallmark of Bank of England notes; a year later, in 1801, the use of waved lines was made exclusive to the Bank by an Act of Parliament.[12] The adoption of this particular design of watermark has been described as the only material outcome of the twenty-five year search for the inimitable note.

As the number of forged notes increased so did the number of suggestions from the public as to how the problem might be combated. Some ideas were exhaustively investigated at not inconsiderable cost to the Bank, while others merited only summary dismissal. Occasionally one proved to be prophetic in what it proposed. The outcome of the search proved the truism that what one man can do another can copy, and exploded the myth of the existence of an inimitable note.

The search for inimitability 1797–1821

Until the advent of the Restriction, forgery of the Bank's notes had been a containable problem; but this had happened more by accident than by design. Occasionally the appearance of forgers such as George Nicholas (who it will be remembered altered the amounts of notes), and Charles Price[13] whose work initially went undetected at the Bank itself, provoked some precautionary measures, but generally things went on as before. All the while the number of notes in circulation was increasing and, in London at least, the Bank of England note was becoming more and more familiar – the Act of 1708[14] prohibiting an association of more than six people to practise banking had ensured a monopolistic position for the Bank and its note issue.

From the early years the Bank had tended to look towards the paper on which its notes were printed to provide the key in the fight against the forger, and there are many instances of this happening: in 1694, for example, when running cash notes were to be printed on 'marbled paper indented';[15] in 1697 when Rice Watkins was commissioned to supply special paper which carried the Bank's own watermark;[16] and in 1724 when the long association with Portals began, probably as a result of George Nicholas' criticism two years before of the Bank's note paper.[17] This preoccupation with paper, commendable though it was, could only ever represent a part-solution: paper was only one of the three components comprising a note, the others being ink and design, and of the ink the Committee of the Society of Arts had commented in their report in 1819 that '. . . In this respect the Bank of England Note seems to be nearly perfect . . .'[18]

With design, however, it was a different story. Developing from goldsmiths' notes the graphic design of the Bank's had undergone no radical changes and had merely been altered piecemeal. Had greater cognisance been taken of advances in printing technology and the style of lettering, had sum piece and vignette been reworked with perhaps more imagination and vigour and less deference to precedent, then an escape might have been made from the 'variation on a theme' concept that had simply evolved through the pragmatism of the previous one hundred years. Certainly this conservatism or reluctance to change was one of the contributory factors which had led inexorably to the too-easily-forged low denominations of the Restriction Period.

Although the public's initial reaction to the stoppage of cash payments

The Bank's copy of Alexander Tilloch's 1797 design.
(195 × 115 mm)

Machine ruled design by William Bawtree, the Bank's engraver, 1821. (175 × 115 mm)

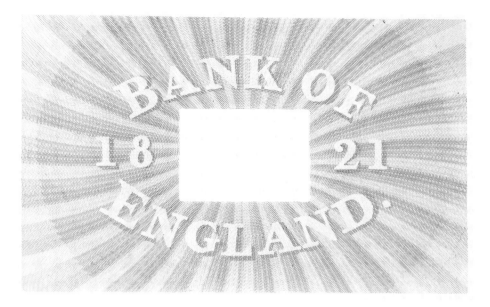

had been one of unease (and at this stage it was still mainly a London-based public) its fears were allayed by the terms of the declaration signed by more than 4,000 people, headed by the Lord Mayor and leading London traders, that they would accept bank notes for any payment due to them and would make their payments in the same way.[19] It was a pragmatic blend of patriotism and practicality.

As well as issuing one and two pound notes to alleviate the shortage of currency the Bank also sold captured Spanish Dollars or eight reale coins – the notorious 'pieces of eight'. These coins had been held in the vaults purely for their bullion value and when stamped with a small oval containing a likeness of George III on the neck of the Spanish monarch, Charles IV, could be bought by the public at 4s/9d each. It inspired the couplet:

> The Bank to make their Spanish dollars pass
> Stamped the head of a fool on the neck of an ass.

and drew the cynical comment: 'Two Kings' heads and not worth a crown'. Yet these coins together with the low denomination notes filled a desperately-felt gap and in one sense formed the provender for the 'nation of shopkeepers'.

An interesting sidelight on the social acceptability of paper money after the stoppage appeared in *The Gentleman's Magazine* in June 1797.[20] That journalistic bastion of England's upper middle class, who in tune with the social mores of the age, harboured a distaste for commerce and all that it entailed, recorded with a wry smile that:

In a small yew-tree in the garden of Mr Samuel Warburton, of Sheffield, a wren, a linnet and a blackbird have built their respective nests. These little musical tenants

45

of the tree live in perfect harmony together, and, according to the fashion of the times, pay their rents to Mr Warburton in notes.

The Bank had always been alive to the threat that forgery of its notes might pose: if the number grew too large people might become over-wary and reluctant to handle them which, in its turn, could lead to a loss of confidence in the Bank itself. Confidence or trust is, of course, the cornerstone of banking and a loss of confidence could strike at the very vitals of the Bank and therefore the official pocket of the nation into which the government was accustomed to dip. This public attitude (and indeed this did happen with its small notes outside London) is well illustrated in a letter Robert Southey wrote from Bristol in July 1803. He observed, 'Our market folk this day unanimously refuse to take the small Bank of England bills. Bristol paper they receive without hesitation'. In his *Letters from England* published under the guise of a Spanish nobleman he explains the preference:

I can plainly see that every person dislikes these small notes . . . You are always in danger of receiving forged ones . . . but the country bankers, whose credit depends upon fair dealing, pay their forged notes, and therefore provincial bills are always preferred in the country to those of the Bank of England.[21]

The provincial preference for provincial notes can possibly be partly attributed to local loyalties – many bore engravings of familiar local landmarks – but it was more likely to be due to the fact that the country banks' notes were less susceptible to forgery. In some respects the small size of country bankers' issues enabled them to indulge in producing high quality notes by methods which could not be used to produce notes in the quantities needed by the Bank. Also their notes often circulated in localised areas and so would be identified as forgeries sooner. Having said that, however, there were of course forgeries of country bank notes but they were often paid as genuine as Southey says. The pragmatic country banker, realising that it was in his interests to avoid the risk of losing the confidence of his local customers, tended to pay without protest.

With the Bank of England's notes the scale of the problem was entirely different. They circulated freely in London at least – and in passing unremarked so gave the utterer (the legal term for the person who puts forgeries into circulation) the anonymity he needed. In 1807, the year that *Letters from England* was published, the total circulation of the Bank's notes varied between £15.5 and £24.5 million of which one and two pound notes accounted for an average total of around £4.7 million.[22] During that year 3,016 one-pound and 1,123 two-pound notes were found to be forged when presented at the Bank's counters. Other denominations were forged too, but apart from the number of five-pound notes – in 1807 it was 384 – the balance was negligible, hardly altering during the rest of the Restriction and actually showing a fall when cash payments were resumed.[23]

Proposal by Jacob
Perkins.
(195 × 125 mm)

Towards the end of 1797 it was apparent that forgery of the newly-introduced one and two pound denominations was becoming a serious problem and, if anything, was likely to increase; suggestions were invited from the public as to how the Bank's notes might be made more forgery-proof and the search for the inimitable note began.

Almost four hundred suggestions were received over a period of twenty-five years. Many were completely impracticable, such as Richard Hughes' proposal in 1812 to have the number incorporated in the watermark of each note, while others, such as that of Mr W. Morgan, 'that a Portrait of the King, engraved in the line way, by the best Engraver, should be printed on all Bank Notes' proved to be way ahead of their time.[24]

From May 1797 until February 1802 the public's suggestions were considered by the Committee of Treasury, the senior standing committee of the Bank's Court of Directors. Consisting of the Governor, Deputy Governor and the more senior Directors it has been described as 'the nucleus of the Bank's energy'.[25] The fact that the Bank was prepared to devote important resources to this problem was evidence of the seriousness with which it was viewed; but it was also eminently sensible that those who ultimately had to approve whatever anti-forgery devices and other changes were introduced to the Bank's own notes should hear first-hand the views of others on the subject.

Alexander Tilloch, a London printer, was the first to submit a proposal. In May 1797 he presented an engraving to the Committee which, he stated, could not be imitated; although it was, in fact, of rather poor quality.[26] The Committee, adhering to the dictum that what one man can do another can copy, set the Bank's engraver, Garnet Terry, the task of 'forging' the Tilloch note which had been engraved in relief for surface printing. Although his copy was in recess on a copper plate, Terry's work satisfied the Committee, who decided '. . . Mr Terry, the engraver of Bank Notes having imitated it very nearly, Mr Tilloch's Plan was not adopted'. Declaring that the copy was nowhere near a passable imitation Tilloch retired in rancorous mood, but was to re-enter the arena some twenty years later when it became clear that he had behaved less than honestly.[27] Other suggestions included one 'that Bank notes be wrought in silk'[28] but the Committee decided that such notes 'would not answer for the operations and services of the Bank'. Indeed several ideas revolved around this element of notes – using coloured paper, impressing or raising certain parts of the paper to signify the value of the note and so on. This was a familiar avenue for the Bank bearing in mind the new waved line watermark introduced in 1801 which eventually did have some impact on the number of forgeries.

Some ideas were brusquely dismissed with the curt comment that 'the Committee thought they would be impractical and ineffectual' and it is difficult not to sympathise with the Committee who must sometimes have suffered at the hands of cranks; the expectation of financial reward also brought out the time-wasters; indeed the Court of Directors remarked in a report of 1818 that 'the plans of those persons who stipulated in the first

Design in red, black and white by Sir William Congreve, 1821.
(185 × 115 mm)

Design by Perkins,
Fairman and Heath
from hardened steel
plate.
(190 × 105 mm)

instance for remuneration, proved, of all others, the least deserving of notice'.[29] But amongst the schemes that would obviously not lend themselves to the mass-production required and those which replicated ideas already considered and put aside (the phrase, '. . . was thanked for his communication and acquainted, that a similar plan had been in contemplation' occurs frequently), there is the occasional germ of an idea which the Bank would have done well to investigate further. Perhaps the Committee was looking for the complete and perfect answer from a single source? With hindsight there certainly seem to be scattered amongst the proposals ingredients which when conjoined might well have provided the answer to the problem.

Meanwhile several changes were being made to the design of the two lowest denominations. We have already described how the 1797 issue of one and two pound notes was replaced a year later with a new design in which the printed area was much reduced and the denomination in letters printed at the centre top. In 1801, the same year that the waved line watermark came into use, the design of these two denominations reverted to using the full area of the paper. Refinements such as printing the denomination of the one pound note in italic and that of the two pound in Gothic script were tried. The sum pieces of the two notes had from the beginning been given reasonably distinctive outlines, perhaps to assist the illiterate, and the canted sum piece of the two pound might also have been done for that reason, but there is no evidence to support the supposition. Another feature introduced a little later in 1805, which again might have helped the illiterate, was the vertical line

I.

Proof £1 note of the Northumberland Bank printed from a copper plate engraved by Thomas Bewick early in the 19th century. CM 1983–11–9–170. (217 × 135 mm)

printed across the two pound note, although it was put there for a quite different purpose – to serve as a guide when notes were cut in half and sent by different posts.[30]

Returning to the Bank's quest for the inimitable note, the Committee of Treasury had considered thirty-five ideas by the beginning of 1802. The new notes on the specially-watermarked paper had been issued only in the previous July and had, as yet, had no impact on the forgery problem and so in February 1802 a special committee was appointed '. . . to examine plans for the Improvement of Bank Notes'. During its life of just over a year the Committee examined twenty suggestions. Several, such as using silk,[31] had already been proposed and rejected but others were of more than passing interest. An outstanding engraver who became involved in the campaign for a new note was Thomas Bewick in Newcastle. Although Bewick is revered now for his wood-engravings, he was first apprenticed to, and later worked in partnership with Ralph Beilby, who did much metal-engraving, including some for bank notes. Evidently Bewick enjoyed this line of work, for he recalled in his *Memoirs* that in the 1790s he was interrupted in his *History of British Birds* by:

various other jobs in the Wood Engraving, and also the work of the Shop for my customers in the Town, but particularly, writing Engraving, which I may say I was obliged to learn & pursue after Mr. Beilby left me, and the most interesting part of this kind of work, was plates for Bank notes, checks &c . . .[32]

One guinea note
engraved by Bewick
for the Carlisle Banking
Company, draped with
a floral garland and
lettering composed
of delicate reeds,
reminiscent of details
found in Bewick's
wood-engravings.
CM 1981–11–22–89.
(191 × 142 mm)

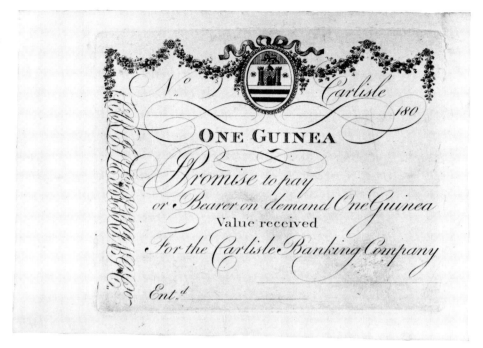

At that time Bewick was invited to engrave a £5 note for the Carlisle Bank; this he did, endeavouring to copy the effect of a wood cut. The technique was admired by Samuel Thornton at the Bank of England, who wrote to Bewick asking how it was done. Interestingly Bewick believed that although his design was appropriate for country banks 'it would not do for the Bank of England'; in this he showed a sharper awareness than many other artists of the different needs of the Bank and her country cousins. However when a Royal Commission was appointed in 1818 to consider ways of preventing forgery, Bewick sent in proposals, wishing 'to contribute all in my power to accomplish so desirable an end.'[33]

Once again he appreciated the practical requirements, and aimed for a device that, firstly, would never need to be altered or repaired; and secondly, would easily be recognised as genuine. His approach is striking both for his own modesty, and his comments on the other plans and the Bank's response. He did not mention the advantages of typography, for example, because he knew it had already been suggested and rejected by the Bank and the Commissioners. 'This to me always appeared strange,' Bewick wrote, 'since, in my opinion there has [sic] been several specimens laid before them perfectly efficient for the purpose of preventing Forgeries, or perhaps totally setting that nefarious work at rest.[34] His own preference was for intricate geometric machine-work, and the more complicated, the better:

The beautifull [sic] specimens first produced by Fairman, Perkins and Heath from their steel plates or blocks, were in my opinion inimitable and quite sufficient to answer the end intended. . . . if an Engine turner cannot set his Lathe, so as to trace or copy the same delicate & truely exact curves & lines &c . . . it is not likely that any forgery will ever be attempted . . . if they had been left complex, I would have liked them better – but as they are, the best Engravers on either Copper, Steel or wood, will not attempt an imitation – they may indeed gaze at them – *but that is all* . . .[35]

We know that the Bank had been discouraged by unsuccessful experiments with reproducing steel-plates, and that they were most attracted by simple designs. Bewick might have understood this reasoning, even if he did not agree with it; what he and many others found incredible was the rejection of all possible improvements in favour of the old, inadequate design:

When I read, in a Newspaper . . . 'that the Commissioners were of opinion *that nothing better than the old Bank note could be devised to prevent forgery*!!! then indeed, on reading this, I could scarcely believe my own Eyes – my astonishment was complete – and my opinion of the whole business of this Mountain in labour was fixed.[36]

Bewick for example brought in an example of wood-engraving recommending that this technique be used, but as usual Terry was able to copy it '. . . by Copper Plate Engraving, and Mr Bewick's Plan was not adopted'.[37] Bewick[38] was the first major artist in this medium (i.e. wood-engraving) which, unlike woodcuts which were made on the side grain of the wood with a knife, was achieved on the end-grain with engraving tools. Very fine work could be produced, but the great advantage of it was that it did not need to be printed separately from letter press. It was developed at the beginning of the nineteenth century, quickly became the most common form of illustration and then equally swiftly disappeared with the advent of photography.

The predominant target amongst these suggestions was paper again. Nine touched on that subject including one from Garnet Terry himself who produced samples of paper in which gold leaf, silk and worsted had been introduced but the Committee remained unconvinced. They must have felt that the new paper with its technologically advanced design of waved lines and, in the case of one and two pound notes, the denomination also incorporated in the watermark, represented the state of the mould and paper makers' art.

The number of forgeries finally fell as the effect of the new paper was felt.[39] The Special Committee stood down having reported that they were satisfied with the paper being used and the notes being issued. As to the proposals they had considered so far, they believed all could be copied easily enough to deceive the man in the street.

The search continued with the Committee of Treasury returning to the task of examining proposals but often the path looked depressingly familiar and without an end in sight. A Mr Williamson, who brought in a plate claiming it to be inimitable because it had been engraved by '. . . an

Instrument', had to acknowledge that Terry's copy was good enough to fool the public.[40] Two suggestions concerned 'secret marks' but although this device was already being used it was no great help in the fight against the forger, because as the marks were secret, notes could only be verified at the Bank, and this of course allowed them to circulate beforehand. Then as now, the public is the first line of defence in the fight against the forger and therefore the principle the Bank was following, a simple familiar image which could not be easily imitated, seemed to be the right one. Robert Southey in his *Letters from England* had clear views on the forgery problem generally and secret marks in particular. On the answer to forgery he succinctly wrote 'What is required is something so obvious that a common and uninstructed eye shall immediately perceive it'.[41] It was precisely the Bank's goal. Secret or 'private' marks as he called them were dismissed with the comment that '. . . as they are meant to be private, [they] can never enable the public to be upon their guard'. There is one other proposal in the period up to 1817 that must be mentioned. It came from an American, J.C.Dyer, who suggested that the Bank's notes should be engraved on steel as the 'New England Notes for Dollars are executed, which had never been forged', but the Bank's engraver – this time it was Terry's successor, J.H.Harper – copied part of the American note 'in a very exact and satisfactory manner'.[42] Despite this the Bank's interest had been aroused by the technique of steel engraving and Dyer was asked to supply steel plates and a press for the Bank's Printing Department to experiment upon.

Sadly Harper's report was not encouraging: the work of engraving the plates took much longer than with copper and the hardening process produced unacceptable blemishes on the unengraved areas. Arguing for the old system he stated that he had found that steel plates could only be used for 35,000 impressions but that a copper plate, which took only one quarter of the time to engrave, would give 15,000[43] impressions, and considerably more if re-touched.[44] Again with hindsight it is easy to see that the changeover from copper to a more durable medium would have to be made sometime. Production techniques needed to keep pace with the public's appetite for notes and at the same time to supply ones which had a distinctive identity and 'sameness'.

At this point it is convenient to retrace our steps slightly and examine three factors which had some impact on the Bank's notes. The first concerns Abraham Newland, that grand old man of the Bank, who had held the post of Chief Cashier for almost thirty years until his retirement in 1807. Because his name had appeared as the payee[45] on all the Bank's notes from 1782 until his retirement it became, not surprisingly, familiar to the public, who nicknamed them 'Abraham Newlands' or sometimes simply 'Newlands'. A popular song with, appropriately enough for the time, patriotic verses was written by Charles Dibdin, Junior.[46]

The dating and numbering of notes by hand was a tedious business for the Bank's clerks, and so when Joseph Bramah demonstrated a hand-operated machine which could number and date 2,000 notes per day by surface printing (as against the 400 maximum that a clerk with pen and ink could manage), the Bank was understandably very interested. Eventually thirty double machines which could handle two notes at a time were ordered.[47] Caslons cast the type which, because of its timeless design, appeared on the Bank's notes until 1945, and a stereotype provided the dateline. The promissory clause was overprinted with the number in two places, and the date also appeared twice with 'London' in between. The Bank had stumbled on an effective anti-forgery device using two printing techniques – the main body of the note in intaglio and the number and date in letterpress. It was effective because the overprinting made alteration difficult, and the printing of the numbers meant that a forger either had to cast his own type to use in conjunction with his plate or suffer the consequences of engraving his copper plate with one number and date which would quickly become known.

The third factor affecting the notes was that in 1812 the sum piece (or sum block), the white letters on a black background which proclaimed the denomination of each note, was reserved by Act of Parliament for the Bank's

Abraham Newland, Chief Cashier of the Bank 1778–1807. Because of his name appearing in the payee clause Bank of England notes acquired the nickname of 'Newlands'. (See the illustration on page 42.) From the painting by George Romney.

A £2 note (of the third design) dated and numbered by one of Joseph Bramah's presses.
(200 × 113 mm)

exclusive use,[48] causing a number of country banks to modify their note designs. Unfortunately neither this nor Bramah's machine actually caused a drop in the number of forgeries; but it is not unreasonable to suppose that what they did do was to contain the problem. Without them it could have grown out of control.

It has been said that in 1817 there were some ten thousand engravers in this country capable of producing an engraving of a Bank of England note.[49] Some years earlier Robert Southey had described the unemployment and consequent want of ' . . . so many ingenious mechanics . . .' in Birmingham. He opines that '. . . there is more excuse to be made for dishonesty in Birmingham, than could be pleaded any where else', and goes on 'It is not to be expected but they will patiently be starved, if by an ingenuity of their own they can save themselves from starving.'[50] Bearing Southey's observations in mind it comes as a surprise to learn that probably no more than ten plates were responsible for the large number of forgeries, and that they seem mainly to have originated from the Birmingham area. Furthermore it seems that there may well have been a well-organised system for slipping these notes into circulation: a small nucleus of forgers supplied wholesalers of notes who in their turn sold them to the retailers with the utterer at the end of the line.

The public's anger when the grim statistics of the forgery prosecutions became known, led to the recall in 1817 of the Bank's Special Committee which had examined 'plans for the Improvement of Bank Notes' during 1802–3.[51] Parliamentary questions and a request in 1816 for a return of the numbers of forged notes presented at the Bank over the previous four years had helped to bring the facts to the public's attention. The result was an influx of suggestions, hence the revival of the Special Committee. This growing public concern in what was after all a public problem led to the appointment of a Royal Commission of Inquiry and provoked the Society of Arts into suggesting possible solutions.

As before, the *modus operandi* of the Special Committee was to have the Bank's engraver copy any proffered samples of 'inimitability'. One proposal requiring three types of engraving – one by machine, the others by hand – was rejected as impractical for large-scale production because of the different rates of wear between hand- and machine-engraved plates. The promoter, Edward Scriven, when confronted with this decision insisted on a copy being made of the machine-engraving, which Harper did, and Scriven acknowledged it was closer to the original than he expected.[52] Another machine-engraving proposal came from J.L.Bradbury who, accompanied by his sponsor Mr P.Moore MP, sought funds to finance some research work. It was refused and eventually Bradbury and Moore returned with examples of machine-engraving '. . . very inferior to what others had produced . . .' which again, was successfully copied '. . . so closely that Mr Moore expressed himself thoroughly satisfied'. But this did not stop Moore making, as the contemporary summary of the proposals goes on to record, '. . . a representation totally different in his place in the House of Commons'.[53] Of the other suggested solutions, which rather prophetically included micro-printing and printing the backs of notes by lithography, there was one, in 1818, which unexpectedly found favour with the Committee and attracted their support. In rather vague terms Augustus Applegath and his partner Edward Cowper, suggested a general concept which corresponded with the Bank's perception of how inimitability, or rather something close to it, might be achieved. As far as the Bank was concerned this inimitability had two aspects: firstly its notes should be familiar to the public, who because of this familiarity should be enabled to recognise a genuine note with ease; and secondly it should be technologically advanced enough to deter the most determined forger. Applegath's idea of simple impressions to 'enable the Public to protect themselves . . . to make but little alteration in the face of the Bank Note, and to fill the reverse with appropriate engraving'[54] was precisely what the Committee wanted to hear. In May it was agreed to advance £1,200 to the partners so that they could develop their plan further.[55] On the design aspect Applegath used a simple formula to good effect. It consisted of a Britannia on either side of the note, a large centrally-placed panel that contained the denomination in words and divided the promissory clause, all headed by 'Bank of England', again, in a panel. It was a design that he varied as his experiments progressed. Early proofs were monochrome but later ones used as many as five colours. But the masterstroke was that the back of the note bore a perfect mirror image of the front. This was made possible by the adaptation of his partner Cowper's recent (1816) invention of a machine for printing wallpaper which

Plate 1

(*Right*) One guinea note issued by the Royal Bank of Scotland in 1777.
It was the first British note to be printed in three colours.
CM 1986–5–9–1.
(137 × 128mm)

(*Below*) Original artwork for a £100 note of the Royal Bank of Scotland, *c.*1854–61, incorporating a red overlay to be printed by lithography.
CM 1984–11–16–1.
(205 × 125mm)

Plate 2

Unissued design for the Bank of England by Applegath and Cowper. The design on the back was a reversed impression of that upon the front and in register with it, an anti-forgery device suggested by a forger incarcerated in Newgate 100 years before.

£1 note of the Darlington Bank, dated 1814, embellished with colour printing and a detailed vignette. CM 1981–11–22–138. (189 × 88mm)

Plate 3

(*Right*) A British Linen
Company £1 note of 1893,
printed by Perkins, Baker &
Co. in blue with a red
lithographic overlay.
It typifies the design and
colour of late 19th-century
Scottish bank notes.
CM 1982–9–25–2.
(150 × 124mm)

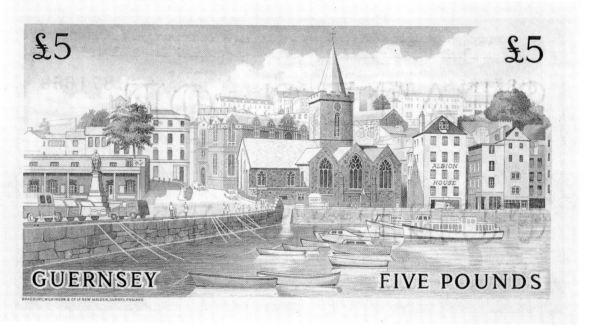

A harbour scene on the back of a States of Guernsey £5 note of 1969 printed in muted pastel colours. CM 1984–6–5–339.
(146 × 84mm)

Plate 4

(*Above*) Farm girl and Jersey cattle on the back of a States of Jersey 10 shilling note of 1942, designed by the local artist Edmund Blampied. CM 1984–6–5–322. (129 × 84mm)

(*Right*) River mask representing the River Blackwater on the back of a 10 shilling note of the Central Bank of Ireland, dated 1968. (detail) CM 1983–11–9–249. (whole note 137 × 77mm)

using stereotypes bent round the cylinders, was able to print 1,200 notes per hour. Perfect registration was obtained simply by offset printing of the back of the note from a leather pad which had already received the impression from the stereotype. The machine needed to revolve twice to print one sheet: on the first revolution no paper was inserted, and the impression was made on the leather pad; on the second paper was fed in the front, printed, and the back set-off simultaneously.

Whilst Applegath and Cowper were carrying out their secret experiments, the Bank was being castigated by the public for not doing enough to improve the security of its notes: '. . . any boy who had been six months with an engraver might imitate, so well as to make the difference imperceptible, the Notes of the Bank of England' and '. . . a lower degree of art could not exist than was displayed in the preparation of Bank of England Notes' were just two examples of the type of criticism levelled at the Bank. The author of both of these, Sir James Mackintosh, subsequently pressed for a Parliamentary inquiry into the prevention of forgery but in the end it was the Royal Commission that was appointed. The Commission made two reports from its Soho Square premises: the first, published on 22 January 1819, proved to be a vindication of the Bank's actions, hinted at Applegath and Cowper's breakthrough and finished on the overall question urging that '. . . those with whom the responsibility rests, to be fully satisfied that they shall produce an Improvement, before they venture to effect a Change'.[56] In the main body of the Report the Commissioners mentioned that they examined 108 projects which had already been rejected by the Bank, were shown 70 varieties of experimental paper made by Portal and Bridges, and looked at the paper money of other countries. The public, the Commissioners felt, were easily deceived by poor imitations; they deprecated the fact that forgers — and they accepted that they were few in number — were rarely apprehended whilst the luckless utterers were constantly brought to justice. Acknowledging that the Bank was doing everything it could to detect the forgers and recognising the objections against a system of offering rewards they believed, nevertheless, that a large reward might well produce results. They interviewed the Bank's solicitor, Chief Inspector and Chief Investigator and questioned them on how they carried out their duties. The Commissioners' final report published a year later[57] was a very flimsy document which recommended Applegath and Cowper's proposal and did nothing else. All in all there is no doubt that they had been inquiring as much into the part played by the Bank as they had been into the prevention of forgery, and that on the former they could find no fault whilst on the latter they certainly had nothing new to offer.

So far there had only been one serious rival to Applegath and Cowper, an American Jacob Perkins, whose process of 'siderography' was already used in the production of the New England notes in America. Some years before

Specimen note by Jacob Perkins. The repetition of features such as the portrait vignettes and machine-engraved patterns demonstrates the effectiveness of the Plate Transfer Press. (208 × 120 mm)

J.C.Dyer, acting as agent for Perkins, had tried unsuccessfully to interest the Bank in this process but technical difficulties encountered over hardening the engraved steel plates had led to its rejection. This time Perkins came to London to present the proposal himself.[58] In the process a steel plate was engraved, hardened, and then used as the master die from which the printing plates were made by means of a Plate Transfer Press or 'check plate' as Perkins described it. There were three important advantages to Perkins' scheme: it ensured identity of the notes through the plate transfer press, longevity of the plates because they were of hardened steel, and security through intricate machine-engraving. It is difficult to understand why the Bank did not adopt such an excellent scheme straightaway because in 1832, only eleven years after it had been all but rejected, the Bank's Deputy Governor was enthusiastically reporting on the Bank of Ireland's printing methods which included, ironically enough, a Plate Transfer Press.

Applegath and Cowper's association with the Bank ended abruptly in September 1821 when the Bank's engraver (by now Harper had retired and been replaced by William Bawtree) satisfied the Special Committee with his copy of the partners' latest note which used five colours. The Bank had invested money and resources in the project: secure accommodation for the printing process had been provided within the Threadneedle Street building itself, and even a steam engine to drive the partners' machinery; also the Bank's papermakers, Portal and Bridges, had gone to the expense of installing special machinery to make paper to Applegath's specification. Sadly all their efforts and the faith placed in them by the Bank had come to naught because of the invariable test: their product could be copied. They were paid compensation and departed.[59]

It may be that the underlying reason for the failure of both the Perkins and Applegath schemes can be linked with the resumption of cash payments or convertibility. The Bank had wanted a return to paying its notes in cash for some years and had made representations to Parliament to that effect; convertibility had been regarded as a possibility in 1816 and then again in 1818 but on each occasion had had to be postponed. Eventually Peel's Act of 1819 allowed payments in gold to be made at any time from 1 May 1821 to 1 May 1823.[60] The Bank chose to return to its old ways at the first opportunity and did so on 1 May; at the same time the issue of small notes, introduced as an emergency measure with the imposition of the Restriction in 1797, ceased.

The end of these low denomination notes meant, of course, the end of pressure on the Bank to find a solution to the forgery problem; it had been the forgery of these small notes which had sparked off the search for inimitability.

The public campaign

In 1819 the Society of Arts reported that 'the rapid increase, during the last three or four years, of convictions before the criminal courts for the circulation of Forgeries of the Bank of England Notes, is such as to have made a very serious impression on the public mind.'[61] Licensing the issue of notes for less than five pounds, when coin was so scarce, opened the floodgates for country banks, the numbers of which rose from some three hundred in the late 1790s to well over seven hundred in the 1810s. The restriction on cash payments did not apply to the country bankers; legally they were still obliged to

'A peep into the old rag shop in Threadneedle Street'. Cartoon published 28 September 1818 by S. W. Fores, 50 Piccadilly. An unfortunate has been brought to the Bank accused, presumably, of an offence connected with forgery; but the officials are unable, because of the poor quality of the Bank's notes, to decide whether it is forged or not.

redeem their notes in coin, but in practice they simply offered Bank of England notes. Some banks even printed this on their notes: for example, five guinea and one guinea notes of the Thirsk Bank, dated 1809 and 1810, say 'I promise to pay the Bearer on Demand . . . in Bank of England notes or Cash.' As a result, there was a considerable increase in the number of bank notes generally, and in particular, in the geographical reach of Bank of England notes.

Paper money was not only now used by more people; it was used by different people. As the Society of Arts said, 'It is evident that the currency of lowest denomination, whether that be metallic coin or promissory paper, must be that which circulates chiefly among the lower classes, and for the payment of small sums.'[62] The new one and two pound notes brought paper money into the hands of precisely the people least able to understand and trust it, and most vulnerable to fraud. From the public's point of view the campaign for a new note was almost a moral and philanthropic issue, a demand for social reform. Many people felt that the penalties of transportation or death, even for just passing a forged note, were severe out of all proportion to the crime. To many it seemed unfair that ordinary people should pay the price for having genuine difficulties in coping with an unfamiliar type of money, which, in the absence of coin, was virtually forced upon them.

Underlying the whole controversy was the fundamental question of whether paper money was an acceptable alternative to gold, and to this extent, it involved all banks, not just the Bank of England. A cartoon published in 1810, called 'The Ghost of a Guinea . . . or the Country Banker's Surprise!!' shows an astonished banker staring at a mirage of coins and exclaiming, 'I declare I have not seen such a thing since I have been in the Banking line . . .' In 1818 a skit note, engraved as competently as many genuine bank notes, promised to pay 'Messrs. Fudge, Swindle and Nocash, Bankers . . . TWO PENCE, when country banks shall have been abolished and when Sterling GOLD and SILVER, only, shall again become the circulating medium of Old England.' From the outbreak of the war with France in 1793, many banks faced runs of panic-stricken customers trying to exchange their notes for coin, and could only save their reputation and business by calling on influential and wealthy customers to state publicly their faith in the bank's stability. These public advertisements probably gave little comfort, however, to the poorer customers. William Forbes, a successful Scottish banker, recorded that all the Edinburgh bankers met in March 1797, and decided to follow the Bank of England's lead in stopping cash payments. At once Forbes found his counting-house filled with 'the lowest and most ignorant classes, such as fishwomen, carmen, street-porters and butchers' men, all bawling out at once for change.'[63] There was nothing pejorative about Forbes' use of the word 'ignorant'. He was simply describing what he saw: uneducated people did not trust bank notes.

Illiterate people could be deceived by skit notes like this Fort Montague 5 half-pence note of 1794, which could pass for 5 pounds. CM 1980—11—30—137. (182 × 120 mm)

Although all bankers were affected, the Bank of England bore the brunt of the anger. C. W. Williams, writer of a pamphlet published in 1818, observed that in many people's minds 'the Bank is charged with indifference to the cries of humanity at the heart-rending catalogue of persons tried and executed for the crime of forgery.'[64] In fact this pamphlet was published after the Bank had begun sponsoring Applegath and Cowper to design a new note, and the author himself did credit the Bank Directors with 'some compassion' but he warned bluntly that twenty years of merely considering solutions was not good enough, for 'This unprofitable incubation will no longer satisfy the public.'[65]

In an age when cheap prints and satirical engravings were a popular medium for spreading news and propaganda, artists and engravers were able to use their skills to ridicule the new notes, and, appropriately, the poor quality of their engraving. An unequivocal social message was contained in Abraham Franklin's 'Bank Restriction Barometer' which showed a scale of the respective benefits and evils of payments in gold and the bank note system. The consequences of the latter were unremitting disaster, emotively described: no gold, more paper, higher prices, inadequate wages, and 'industry reduced to Indigence, broken-spirited, and in the Workhouse; or, endeavouring to preserve independence, lingering in despair, committing suicide, or dying broken-hearted.' High on the scale appeared the increased temptation to forge Bank of England notes, resulting in 'Frequent and useless inflictions of the barbarous Punishment of Death.' The 'Barometer' sold for one shilling, along with George Cruikshank's 'Bank Restriction Note', probably the most famous satire on the cash suspension. The note was a grim caricature of the Bank of England note, bearing skulls and gibbets, and transportation ships surrounding Britannia gobbling infants. The '£' sign was a noose, and the note was signed 'J.Ketch', common slang for the hangman. Along the left-hand side Cruikshank printed sardonically 'Specimen of a Bank Note – not to be imitated.'

While the 'Barometer' demanded nothing less than a return to gold cash payments, Cruikshank concentrated on an end to the death penalty. He claimed to have sketched his note in ten minutes, moved by seeing a woman hanged opposite Newgate Prison for having passed a forged note. 'The fact that a woman could be put to death for such a minor offence had a great effect upon me,' he wrote, 'and I at once determined if possible to put a stop

Abraham Franklin's 'Bank Restriction Barometer', published in 1819, contrasted the evils of inconvertible paper currency with the benefits of payments in gold. CM 1980–3–43–2. (267 × 423 mm)

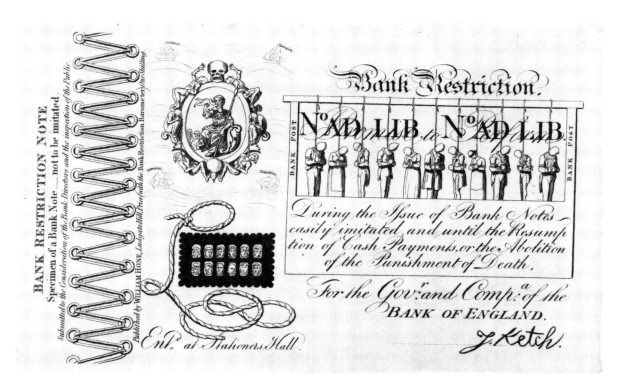

BANK RESTRICTION NOTE

Specimen of a Bank Note — not to be imitated

Submitted to the Consideration of the Bank Directors and the inspection of the Public.

Published by WILLIAM HONE, Ludgatehill, Price 1s the Bank Restriction Barometer, or the Shilling

Bank Restriction.

Nº AD LIB to Nº AD LIB

BANK POST

BANK POST

During the Issue of Bank Notes easily imitated, and until the Resumption of Cash Payments, or the Abolition of the Punishment of Death,

For the Govr. and Compa. of the BANK OF ENGLAND.

J. Ketch.

Entd. at Stationers Hall.

The cartoonist George Cruikshank protested against the severe penalties for forgery by drawing a Bank Restriction Note grimly decorated with skulls, gibbets and a hangman's noose. CM 1980—3—43—1. (207 × 130 mm)

to this shocking destruction of life for merely obtaining a few shillings by fraud.'[66]

This was social campaigning with a modern ring: criminals were victims of the system. The system was hard, for it is quite apparent that not only those who actually perpetrated the forgeries risked dire punishment; anyone who handled the counterfeit notes, knowingly or not, stood to suffer just as much. On the death of a notorious Irish forger, *The Freeman's Journal* reported that 'so extensive was his practice and so numerous were his agents, that it might truly be said he had been the cause of bringing 100 poor wretches to the gallows and contributed more towards peopling Botany Bay than all the other forgers of Ireland put together.'[67] Clearly transportation was the less awful of two dreadful fates, but it was no soft option. In 1806 John Bliss, a Buckinghamshire farmer and innkeeper, was charged 'with having uttered or published divers forged or counterfeited Bank of England Notes; knowing the same to be forged or counterfeited.'[68] Before his trial Bliss spent almost four months in Aylesbury Gaol. According to contemporary descriptions, felons slept in cells 6'6'' by 5' with a wooden bedstead, a straw mattress, and one blanket. They were fed with $1\frac{1}{2}$lbs of bread a day and one pint of soup twice a week.[69] A prisoner of 1800 reported that the prison was in a bad state, and that it was impossible to stay free of vermin. In the spring of 1807 Bliss was sentenced to be transported for fourteen years. Within a month he was sent notice to quit the fields he rented, though his wife was given the chance to take over some of the land. However before he set sail for Australia, Bliss was confined for ten months in the 'Retribution', a notorious prison hulk at Woolwich. Another prisoner recorded his shock on boarding the hulk:

There were confined in this floating dungeon nearly six hundred men, most of them double-ironed; and the reader may conceive the horrible effects arising from the continual rattling of chains, the filth and vermin naturally produced by such a crowd of miserable inhabitants, the oaths and execrations constantly heard among them; and above all, from the shocking necessity of associating and communicating more or less with so depraved a set of beings . . . On descending the hatch-way, no conception can be formed of the scene which presented itself. I shall not attempt to describe it; but nothing short of a descent to the infernal regions can be at all worthy of a comparison with it.[70]

Bliss did not reach New South Wales until December of 1808, when he entered the service of a cattle farmer. Nine years later he received a pardon for good behaviour from the Governor. In April 1817 Bliss at last set sail for England, but after seven months at sea he fell ill and died. He was buried at sea, off the Cape of Good Hope.

Others did not even enjoy a reprieve of eleven years in prison and a foreign land. James Hardy Vaux, a gentleman thief who had his death sentence reduced to transportation, shared a condemned cell with a man convicted of selling forged bank notes, and he included in his memoirs a pitiful account of the fellow's mounting terror. The prisoner, Nicholls, had been betrayed by another agent, and believed that the Bank wished to make an example of him because he had not been willing to save his own life by giving information about the forgers. This bears out the theory that the crime of forgery itself was masterminded by a few ring-leaders, who manipulated and hid behind a much larger number of middlemen, and that the Bank did offer people opportunities to reduce their sentences. When the jailer at last came to confirm that the death sentence would be carried out in a week's time, Nicholls answered in agony, 'I could have wished, Mr. Newman, for a little longer time – I'm not prepared to die – I have some wordly affairs to settle – but – God help me! – I hope for more mercy from him than the Gentlemen of the Bank have shewn me.'[71] On the night before his sentence four companions sat up with Nicholls, reading and singing hymns. This was only of limited comfort, for 'Poor Nicholls was, however, in a very low and desponding state, and evidently dreaded the approach of death . . . At eight o'clock the doleful sound of the tolling bell announced the awful ceremony, and he was a few minutes afterwards launched into eternity.'[72] Nicholls' guilt is not in dispute, but it is easy to see why so many people found the punishment more reprehensible than the crime. As Vaux remembered,

Johnny Bull and his FORGED Notes !! or — RAGS & RUIN in the Paper Currency !!!

Cartoon of 1819 showing John Bull answering accusations of possessing forged notes. Department of Prints and Drawings, British Museum, Dorothy George catalogue of Political and Personal Satires, No. 13197.

'The fate of this unhappy man, who was of a most inoffensive and gentle disposition, and left a large family to bewail his loss, affected me much.'[73]

To make matters worse it was not only deliberate and proven fraud that was the problem. Much distress was caused by the difficulty of distinguishing between genuine and forged notes and there was the dreadful possibility that someone might be wrongfully accused, because it appeared that even Bank of England officials sometimes could not tell for certain if a note were genuine or false. A cartoon published in 1819, the same year as Cruikshank's 'Bank Restriction Note,' showed John Bull being arrested for possession of forged notes. Helplessly, he explains 'I took all these notes in the way of Trade – I can't tell *Bad Good ones* from *Good Bad ones*. Even those who issue them are *frequently mistaken* and have been *deceived by forgeries*. . . .' It could work the other way, too. One of the most attractive proposals for a new note design came from Thomas Ranson, an engraver who was imprisoned for passing a note supposed to be a counterfeit. Ranson managed to appeal, however, and at this second trial, the offending note was now declared to be genuine, with no dispute from the two Bank officials present. With their freedom, and possibly their lives, at stake, it is little wonder that so many

Thomas Ranson's engraving of his wrongful imprisonment for possessing a Bank of England note alleged to be false, but later declared genuine. *By courtesy of the Chartered Institute of Bankers.*

people hated the law and distrusted the new notes. Along with many other artists, Ranson realised that, apart from changing the law relating to forgery, a more positive answer lay in changing the Bank's notes, so that they could not be so effectively copied. So the moral arguments were accompanied by practical experiments for an improved note.

Although the Bank of England was investigating new forms of design and manufacture, and, as we have seen, many artists and inventors responded directly to the Bank's invitation for ideas, not everyone was satisfied with the Bank's handling of the matter. In March 1817 J.T. Barber Beaumont (a miniature painter to the Dukes of Kent and York) sent a proposal to the Bank; it was almost a year before they replied, saying that similar plans had been received, and dismissed as unlikely to be effective. Nonetheless, Beaumont still thought the prevention of forgery was 'attainable in a very considerable degree, if not wholly so,' and he believed that 'If . . . a succession of persons, who are known as men of science or business, suggest similar means of prevention, the reasonable inference . . . is, that opinions so concurring are

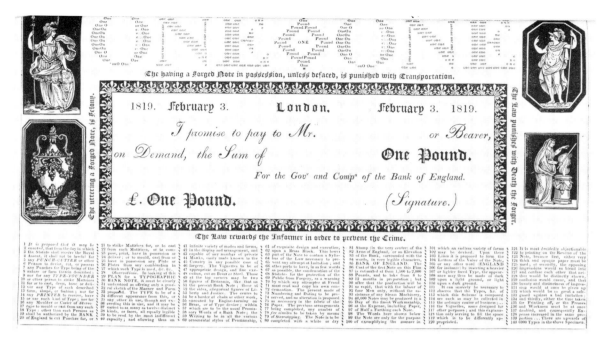

Typographic note design by T.C. Hansard reproduced in the Society of Arts report on preventing forgery.

right.'[74] In March 1818 Beaumont therefore sent a copy of his paper to the Society for the Encouragement of Arts, Manufactures and Commerce and the Society set up its own committee to consider specimen designs and hear evidence from engravers who worked for other banks. Like Beaumont, many of the contributors had already approached the Bank of England without success.

Broadly speaking the submissions to the Society focused on the artistic quality of bank notes, and the technology of their engraving and printing. Although the suggestions for improvement varied, there was virtual unanimity that the Bank of England's notes were sadly lacking in both these aspects. According to Beaumont, technically the notes were of 'inferior workmanship to common engraved shop-bills,' and could be forged 'by any one who can use a camel's hair pencil.'[75] As for content and style, an art dealer, R.H.Solly, felt that the Bank's Directors underestimated the public's capacity for appreciating art: 'I think public bodies should have some regard for the credit of their country. I understand that English art is not much respected on the continent. I hope foreigners do not take the Bank Note for a specimen of English art.'[76]

The designs which the Society reproduced in its published report all recommended major departures in the methods of production of the Bank's notes, to allow more elaborate designs, and to reduce the number of people able to copy them. A popular argument was that several artists and craftsmen should be employed to produce the original plate, as forgers usually worked alone, and no one person would be able to imitate all the different skills. Working on these lines, T.C.Hansard offered a relatively traditional design, which would employ at least twenty people to produce a 'typographic note'. He did suggest some pictorial and ornamental devices: two figures of Britannia, in order to 'preserve wherever it is consistent with my design, any part of the form or feature of the present Bank Note,' were to be engraved in black lines on a white ground, and white lines on black (rather like Applegath's work); and fine writing-engraving would be contained within 'a border of exquisite design and workmanship.'[77] But Hansard's main weapon against forgery was the use of a large variety of typefaces, and particularly Diamond type, the smallest then available. There were, he claimed, only three existing sets of Diamond punches in England, each recognisable to the common eye, and only four or five people in Britain competent to cut new punches. It has already been remarked that eighteenth-century notes sometimes incorporated different styles of lettering; Hansard now followed that principle to hide various 'secret marks' in a panel at the foot of his note, comprising 140 lines of tiny lettering: an italic *d* in line 39, a small capital R in line 44, and so on. By this process Hansard reckoned that 'the learned and the ignorant might be equal judges'[78] of the authenticity of a note, but it is questionable how helpful these minuscule variations in such tiny letters would be to the illiterate.

The major technical innovation recommended in most of the other specimen designs was engraving on steel plates. The revival of the art of steel-engraving, especially for security printing, is widely attributed to the American, Jacob Perkins, who offered his work to the Bank of England, but several British engravers were quick to experiment with this medium. The great advantage of steel was that being a much harder metal than copper, it could give a crisp reproduction of closely shaded lines and detailed engraving, and yield many more thousands of impressions before the plates wore out. In this way the quality of the note designs could be improved, with increased production offsetting the higher costs of the initial engraving. Furthermore, since far fewer people could engrave on steel than copper, the number of potential counterfeiters should be reduced.

As with Perkins' designs, machine-ruling and rose engine work were natural companions for steel plates, taking full advantage of the hard metal to produce extraordinarily complex geometric patterns. The Society of Arts published two spectacular examples of steel-engraving by Richard Williamson, whose claim that the depth of incision possible with steel would produce a more brilliant impression, was admirably demonstrated by patterns of waved lines creating a dazzling play of light and shade. The effect is so vibrant that the patterns almost seem to move before the eyes, and this gives them an air of spontaneity, but Williamson appreciated that for effective security, every new plate must be identical to its predecessors. He therefore assured the

Machine-engraving like watered silk, designed by Richard Williamson for the back of a £10 note of the Monmouth and Abergavenny Bank. CM 1981–11–22–369. (194 × 103 mm)

Richard Williamson's example of dazzling machine-engraving on steel, reproduced in the Society of Arts Report on preventing forgery.

Society that these were not merely 'works of chance', and offered to re-engrave any of his designs to prove it. He estimated that each steel plate should 'assuredly stand 100,000 copies at least.'[79]

Machine-engraving was also featured on the notes submitted by R.H.Solly and Thomas Ranson, who turned to the Society after the Bank had ignored his application. In each case the work of more than one machine-engraver was used for extra security. The central vignette of Solly's note was surrounded by bands of machine-engraving and he claimed that the complexity of the parallel and interlocking lines was such that they would be difficult to copy even with similar machines, let alone by hand. This could, of course, have had disadvantages for the production of new plates, unless something like Perkins' siderography were adopted.

Elegance and allegory in Thomas Ranson's proposed note design: the classical attributes of a cornucopia and Mercury's staff represent fortune and commerce. (detail) CM 1980—3—40—46. (whole note 198 × 123 mm)

In fact both Solly's and Ranson's notes were printed from copper, but Ranson recommended two steel-plates (one for relief, and one for intaglio printing), and Solly used as a vignette a head of Minerva, encircled by a wreath of oak, which had originally been engraved on steel by Charles Warren. This exemplified another benefit of steel, which was the other main thrust of suggestions presented to the Society: namely that the savings of large-scale production would allow greater expenditure on a vignette engraved by a first-class artist.

The effectiveness of fine art as a security measure was by no means a foregone conclusion. Neither Hansard nor Williamson laid much store by it, Williamson rather ridiculously claiming that the poor engraving on a false note might be disguised by blotting ink over the vignette! More serious criticism came from those who believed that the cost of a good engraving would be wasted on a public too ignorant to appreciate the difference between good and bad art. This patronising view was vividly expressed by C. W. Williams, in his pamphlet addressed to the Royal Commission in 1818: 'To talk of taste, or the display of genius to the public, or to expect that such can be appreciated, . . . would be to throw pearls to swine:— it is to expect the admirers of the sports of Bartholomew Fair should become pit critics and literati.'[80] Consequently, Williams concluded that on notes 'The use of fine art alone would be like the use of a different language.'[81]

Of course, the definition of good taste is perennially shifting, as those who claim to possess such a virtue have little desire to devalue it by ascribing it to too many others. Not surprisingly members of the Society of Arts, itself created the previous century to encourage a growing interest in art, were more generous with their gifts, and did not share Williams' high-handed attitude. Solly willingly admitted that the public were not connoisseurs of fine art, but this was no insult, given his view of connoisseurs, who, he said, 'estimate the value of a work solely by its scarcity, or by some arbitrary standard established by a whim or caprice of those who wish to set themselves

R.H. Solly's proposed note design, with a head of Minerva by Charles Warren reproduced in the Society of Arts report on preventing forgery.

up as leaders of the public taste.'[82] The public could, he believed, see the difference between a good work of art and a bad one, but they could only judge what they saw. If a work of fine art were introduced to the Bank of England's notes, the public would soon appreciate its superiority over the existing design.

Naturally many members of the Society of Arts were artists with a vested interest in promoting their profession, but presumably, too, they knew their audience. John Barber Beaumont was in no doubt about the widespread popularity and economic viability of skilled engraving:

And the public are not so insensible of talent in the arts as is often supposed. Publishers are well aware of the interest which the multitude take in a well-executed print, and, therefore, give a high price to superior engravers for embellishments to cheap editions of plays and novels. They would not go to this expense, if the public were insensible to the difference between good and bad engraving.[83]

Beaumont envisaged no less than one third of the face of the Bank of England notes devoted to 'masterpieces of the best historical engravers.' Only another artist of equal calibre would be able to make a convincing copy, and even then, he believed, the different individual style would reveal a different hand. It is perhaps doubtful how many lay people could distinguish such details of style, but as Beaumont pointed out, it was in any case highly unlikely that a first-rate artist would be tempted to crime, as most were too busy with honest employment. Just how high the standard of artwork could be was shown in the centrepiece of Ranson's design, a sumptuous allegorical scene engraved by Ranson from a picture specially painted by John Thurston,[84] which might easily have graced the pages of one of the new illustrated books. While few of the contributors to the Society relied solely on art as a preventative measure, most considered it an essential element of the note design in combination with machine-work and improved means of production.

The Society of Arts did not confine its investigation to hypothetical new designs for the Bank of England. It also considered the evidence and experiences of engravers who produced notes for other banks. Not surprisingly most were full of praise for the country notes, insisting that they were scarcely, if ever, forged, and this largely because of their high-quality engravings. Beaumont said that 'several country Bankers have long been aware of the utility of having their notes engraved in a superior manner, in order to increase the difficulty of imitation.'[85] The engravers' enthusiasm must be received with a little caution: country bank notes were not altogether immune from forgery, and that they suffered less than the Bank of England was partly due, as R.H.Solly realised, to the fact that the former had a much more limited, and local, circulation. But there is no need to be too cynical. Other bankers were often more adventurous than the Bank of England in their choice of note design and the engravers did speak from experience. Richard Silvester, for example, could claim to have engraved plates for almost a

A Chester Bank £1
note of 1810 engraved
by R. and E. Williamson
with a sunray of
machine-ruling similar
to a design submitted
by Richard Williamson
to the Bank of England.
CM 1981–11–22–95.
(180 × 105 mm)

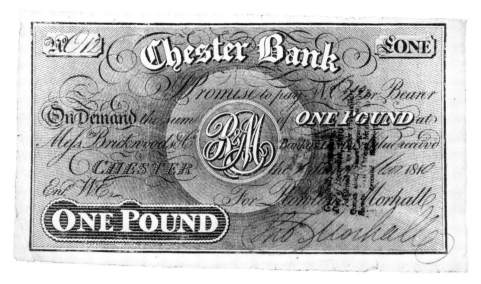

hundred banks, while Harry Ashby had been in business for over twenty years, and in that time worked for forty banks at the very least, and probably a lot more.

The provincial note most recently quoted to the Society of Arts was that of the Plymouth Dock Bank, which found its notes forged after replacing its vignette by Charles Warren with a merely ornamental cypher. They immediately commissioned Warren to produce a new vignette, and the counterfeits ceased. Richard Williamson backed up his proposals by citing his work for the Monmouth Bank, and for notes of banks at Bath and Waterford using his technique for coloured engine-engraving.[86] A Chester Bank one pound note of 1810 engraved by Williamson is covered in a background printing of concentric circles and a sunray of wavy lines, very similar to the design turned down by the Bank of England. Solly referred to the Bank of Ireland's notes, engraved by machinery, which was, he understood, 'very effectual in checking forgery'.[87] He also applauded the Bank of Ireland's policy of instructing the public how to recognise genuine and false notes. In contrast the Bank of England apparently relied 'principally upon certain scratches and dots and pecks, and secret marks' which, Solly pertinently observed, 'can be of no guide to the public so long as they really are kept secret.'[88]

Of course ideas submitted to the Society of Arts were almost bound to contain an inherent bias towards the most inventive technology and good artwork: that, after all, is what the Society was all about. A more general survey of the notes actually circulating in Britain at this time would have revealed considerable variation in the quality of design, from the simplest printed tickets to quite advanced security printing. Most of the notes at the simplest end of the scale were those for small amounts. Some, like a five shilling note signed by Joseph Lawson of Delph, with only crudely-engraved leaves for decoration, appear to have been issues by individuals about whom we have little or no information. Perhaps they were issued by shopkeepers to give change, or by small firms to pay their labourers. Not all were badly printed: the five shilling notes issued in 1812 by Thomas Leigh in Earith were simple in design, but professional in production with pleasing formal lettering of a Germanic style and a few restrained flourishes. The actual wording on the notes is evidence of how they were used: Leigh stated that they were 'for the convenience of small change' and prudently allowed three days from the date of issue (filled in by hand) to redeem the notes.

Next in order of complexity are the interesting notes of banks which faithfully copied the notes of the Bank of England, including the much maligned medallion of Britannia. A one pound note of a Torpoint bank, Snow, Rowe and Company, dated c.1806, bears a remarkable similarity in almost every aspect to the Bank of England's notes of the period 1793 to 1809: three dotted lines at the top of the note for the serial number and date; simply the amount 'ONE', not the name of the bank, top centre; the sum piece, and the medallion. There were differences of detail, particularly in these last two features. In 1812 the Bank of England gained the right to exclusive use of its distinctive sum piece, white Gothic letters on a black ground with a beaded edge; other banks therefore often composed their own variations on the theme. The Torpoint note used almost identical Gothic lettering, but in black and placed against a background of black hatching,

The city arms on a Bristol Bank £5 note of 1807, produced by G. Johnson, a local engraver. CM 1980–11–30–51. (whole note 202 × 106 mm)

74

1812 Thomas
Leigh in Earith issued
notes for small change,
decorated with only a
few flourishes and his
initials in a beaded
medallion.
CM PM–417.
(182 × 95 mm)

£1 note of Snow,
Rowe and Company,
Plymouth Dock,
c.1806, almost identical
in design to Bank of
England notes of that
date.
CM 1981–11–22–499.
(192 × 121 mm)

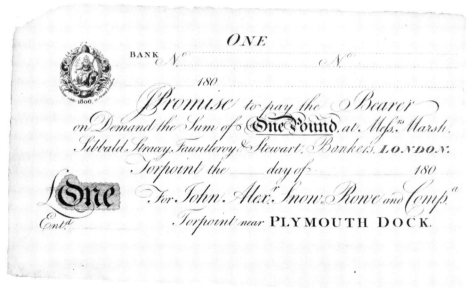

with a scalloped, rather than beaded, edge. The vignette, however, was the
most strikingly similar feature, depicting a seated Britannia holding a branch
of honesty, within a foliated cartouche, under which appeared the date. A
small difference was that the crown at the top of the cartouche on the Bank's
note was replaced by bees buzzing round a hive. The Torpoint note was
engraved by Richard Silvester, who said in evidence to the Society of Arts
that he did not consider Bank of England notes very easy to copy (having
produced the Torpoint note, perhaps he was in a position to judge!), but he
did think that 'they might be made much more difficult of imitation by
employing better artists.'[89] Indeed most of the vignettes Silvester himself

engraved were considerably more delicate in execution and detail than his rendering of the Bank's Britannia, which is curiously at variance with his views and abilities. Perhaps the Torpoint bank particularly requested this design; two other unissued notes of the same period, also engraved by Silvester, suggest that they or he may have had second thoughts. Another design for the one pound note is still traditional, but is in keeping with the best eighteenth-century notes: it is headed with the name 'Torpoint' in ornate lettering with flourishes, carries an attractive monogram resting against an anchor and oak-branch, and overall displays rather more assurance and panache. Silvester's design for a five pound note, however, could hardly present a greater contrast with his 1806 Britannia. Here the note is dominated by a large vignette in which a seated Britannia with spear, shield, helmet and breastplate, presides over the loading of ships at the dockside. She is surrounded by large barrels and packages, symbols of trade, and looks towards an amorphous allegorical figure bearing various classical attributes, who is presumably a messenger of good fortune.

The notes of several country banks during this restriction period show a debt to the Bank of England vignette. A two pound proof note of the West Ham and Essex Bank has a poorly-engraved side view of a seated Britannia, reminiscent of earlier Bank notes. Many banks used a cartouche of stylised foliage to frame their own choice of emblem: for example, a monogram for the Alton Bank, a phoenix rising from the flames at Cirencester, and for the Commercial Bank of Gravesend, a rather charming scene of Neptune in a wheeled chariot, drawn across the waves by two sea-horses.

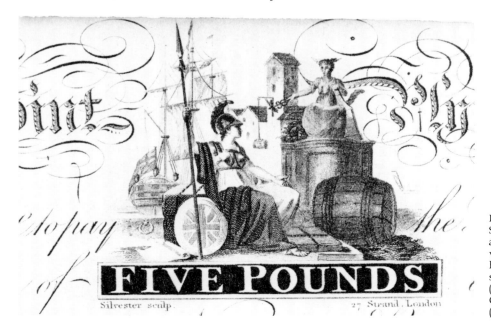

For the £5 note, Silvester produced a more complex vignette of an armed, helmeted Britannia seated at the dockside. (detail) CM 1981–11–22–500. (194 × 120 mm)

Next, there are those banks which displayed more independent spirit in their notes while continuing to pay homage to the broad eighteenth-century format of text with a limited graphic illustration. A design by Harry Ashby for the St Albans Bank bears a shield framed with a pretty naturalistic floral garland, and surmounted by a monogram. Underneath is the local emblem of a stag contained in a circlet with the inscription 'HARTFORDSHIRE'. There are plenty of instances, too, of good work done by provincial engravers. For example, Mark Lambert, a pupil of Thomas Bewick in Newcastle, engraved one pound notes for the Durham Bank, with a Bishop's mitre in the centre of a densely-woven counterfoil scroll pattern. Again following an existing tradition, two Bristol engravers produced rather fine coats of arms for local banks: an elaborate city arms by G. Johnson on notes of the Bristol Bank and the Bristol Bullion Bank, and the Royal Arms by Burnell for the Kingswood Hill Bank.

Country bank notes were often decorated with a foliated cartouche similar to that used by the Bank of England. These examples are from notes of (*from left to right*) the West Ham and Essex Bank, Kettering Bank, the Commercial Bank, Gravesend, and Cirencester Bank.
CM 1981−11−22−665. (196 × 123 mm)
CM 1980−11−30−189. (179 × 92 mm)
CM 1981−11−22−209. (176 × 99 mm)
CM 1981−11−22−98. (200 × 109 mm)

Most notes issued during the period of Bank Restriction probably fall into this third category; attractive, but essentially traditional in design and production. However within this standard format two significant trends appeared, both of which were proposed to the Bank of England, but did not become commonplace until much later. One was printing on the back of notes, an additional opportunity for security printing which also offered scope for pure art and ornament, as the necessary written information was on the front. This might be a pictorial vignette in the centre of the back, like the view of a man fishing in the River Wear with Durham Cathedral in the background, on the back of the Durham Bank one pound note engraved by Mark

(Above) Allegory and civic pride on a 5 guinea note of the Bridgewater and Somerset Bank, dated 1801, engraved by Francesco Bartolozzi, an eminent historical engraver. (detail) CM 1980−11−30−37. (204 × 100 mm)

The Aberystwyth and Tregaron Bank was colloquially known as the 'Black Sheep Bank', after the vignette on its notes. Detail from a £2 note of 1814. CM 1986−10−31−7. (179 × 94 mm)

Back of a Peterborough Bank £5 note of 1817, printed in blue with large ornamental letters and a scroll surrounding the names of the partners and the Bank. CM 1986−10−31−71. (170 × 91 mm)

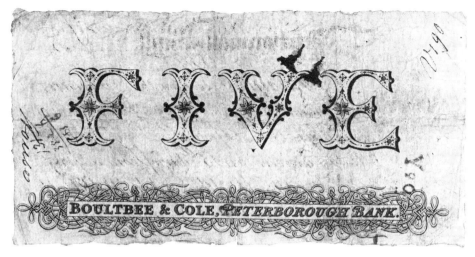

Lambert.[90] Usually, though, printing on the back of notes was restricted to a small panel or scroll framing the partners' initials, the name of the bank, or the denomination written out in words.

The second innovation was colour printing. Limited application of colour to paper money had been tried in Scotland in the 1770s; in 1818 Applegath and Cowper offered the Bank of England geometric patterns vividly printed in up to five colours in perfect register. The country banks could not rise to such complex splendours − probably the method was too unfamiliar, or too expensive, or both; indeed, they did not even go so far as the eighteenth-century examples of notes printed in three colours − black, red and blue. But a number of banks did add one colour to their notes, sometimes by incorporating a few words or designs in colour into the main text on the front of their notes. An added refinement as security against alteration of the value of a note was to use a different colour for each denomination. Ashby's notes for the Berwick Bank in the very early 1800s bore a blue scroll on the five pound note, and a red scroll on the one guinea note. (On the five pound note customers were also reminded of the penalties for fraud with the warning 'NB: To counterfeit is death.') In other instances colour was used only on the back of notes, the front remaining plain black and white, and here, too, the colour could be used to distinguish between denominations. It may well be significant that the same banks (or engravers) who were willing to branch out in one area, also tried their hand in another. Harry Ashby's name appears particularly often on notes with coloured scrolls or designs on the back, or both, often for banks in the North of England. However, it may have also been as much a matter of practicality as of psychology to combine these features, for restricting the colour to an otherwise blank side would allow front and back each to be printed in one operation, thus providing a note

Agriculture represented by a pastoral ploughing scene on a £1 note of 1814 from the Okehampton Bank, by a London engraver, Thorowgood. (detail) CM 1980—11—30—276. (192 × 100 mm)

with two major security features from a relatively simple printing procedure. Red and blue appear to have been the most popular colours, but reverse designs were sometimes printed in brown.

An attractive example of the variety of design elements and printing methods which could be found on country bank notes in this period is a one pound note dated 1814 of the Darlington Bank, engraved by Thorowgood of London. The front carries the traditional text in black script, with a few words, such as the value, printed in red. In the top left-hand corner is a pretty vignette with an allegorical figure representing Agriculture or Plenty, standing against a backdrop of a view of Darlington, still recognisable today. Unusually, the note has two added colours, for the back carries the partners' initials in florid lettering, surmounted by the value and the name of the bank, all printed in blue.

When cash payments for bank notes were restored in May 1821, British paper money embraced a wide spectrum of styles. Ironically the Bank of England notes which sparked so much controversy remained largely unchanged, retaining their familiar, but no longer adequate, eighteenth-century form. At the other extreme was a growing number of country banks experimenting with detailed vignettes, notes printed on both sides and with colour. As many artists and scientists realised, it was these that paved the way for security printing in the future.

The return to gold and the withdrawal of one pound notes temporarily eased the pressure on the Bank of England to re-design its notes, but in the long term there could be no question of clinging to a traditional design too often tried and too little trusted. The vulnerability of the poor and illiterate had been an urgent reason for change, but more sophisticated customers handling higher denomination notes surely deserved protection too; as Beaumont remarked 'As Bank of England Notes are now made, the enlightened and the ignorant are equally disqualified from judging between an original and a copy.'[91] Furthermore, despite the problems and the bad press, people were becoming used to paper money. Vincent Stuckey, who managed a thriving Somersetshire bank, said that in 1816 and 1817 they had been forced to transport coin to London as 'we could not get rid of it in the country, our customers preferring our notes.'[92] He predicted that even when the cash restriction was lifted, people would remember and prefer the convenience of paper.

For the present and the future, then, bank notes had to be secure, to justify and inspire confidence. As many people pointed out, no note could ever be utterly immune to the risk of forgery, because what one person can do, another could copy. But that was no reason for doing nothing. Two realistic goals remained: firstly, to choose a design so distinctive that even if it was copied, people would see the difference; and secondly, to use methods of production which would make forgery expensive and difficult, so reducing the likelihood of it being attempted in the first place. The Society of Arts believed that 'means appear to be accessible to the Bank of England, of rendering the forgery of their notes in a high degree more difficult than at present.'[93] The answer seemed to lie with a combination of skills and technology: engraving on steel to allow large-scale reproduction of both printing-plates and notes for absolute uniformity, used in conjunction with machine-engraving for precision, and good artwork for distinctive and recognisable style. Many of the bank notes printed in Britain in the second and third quarters of the nineteenth century put just these theories into practice.

3 Tradition and innovation

'The old order changeth yielding place to new'.[1]

In 1822 a prominent Manchester Banker, Benjamin Heywood, said in his presidential address to the Liverpool Royal Institution that 'more than any other nation has Great Britain reason to consider with grateful respect the alliance of commerce with science, literature and the arts.'[2] In saying this he paid tribute to a legacy bequeathed by the previous century; even more, he anticipated a fusion of interests that was to dominate the Victorian age. Then, perhaps more than at any other stage in British history, the aims of art, science, commerce and ethics were joined in a common philosophy, each encouraging the other in the search for national dignity and prosperity.

Bankers, no less than any other sector of society, were affected by the split personality of the nineteenth century, for it is one of the less fortunate combinations of historical circumstance that the inexorable processes of industrialisation and urbanisation, which encouraged the growth of banks and paper money, also spawned an inadequately educated working-class, ill-prepared to cope with new ways of handling money. But the same spirit of reform and innovation which helped to maintain the momentum of the industrial revolution also offered solutions to the problems it created. Firstly, legislation to control the organisation of banks and the size of their note circulation helped to protect the public from mismanaged and unstable banks. Secondly, technical innovation and the arts helped in the continuing battle against forgery.

The banking background

After the turmoil of the war years, the return to cash payments in 1821 temporarily eased the pressure on the Bank of England to produce a new note design. But it was only a temporary respite, and for the banking profession as a whole, there were still difficult hurdles to face. As we saw in the last chapter, even problems concerned directly with note design could be caused or at least exacerbated by other circumstances. The public's acceptance of paper money often depended on the reputation of the issuing bank, and this in turn fluctuated at the mercy of the wider commercial climate. Deep-rooted suspicion could not be won over even by the opulent notes of sound banks, as two Manchester partnerships discovered. In 1821 Jones Loyd and Heywood each had plates prepared for new notes but a newspaper report aroused strong local opposition. At a meeting convened by the borough reeve, it was resolved that the notes should only be accepted in extreme necessity, and then not circulated. Not surprisingly the issues were abandoned.

For all bankers the 1820s were challenging years leading to long-term changes. A widespread commercial panic in 1825 resulted in an epidemic of bankruptcies, and by the spring of 1826 over sixty country banks had gone out of business altogether. In an attempt to alter the situation in which, in Lord Liverpool's often-quoted words, 'any petty tradesman, any grocer or cheesemonger, however destitute of poverty might set up a bank in any place,'[3] the Banking Co-partnerships Act was passed in that year, permitting the creation of banks in England and Wales with more than six partners outside a 65-mile radius of London. In 1833 the renewal of the Bank of England's charter contained a clause permitting joint-stock companies in London to act as banks, though they could not issue notes. The principles contained in these acts, i.e. larger bank partnerships, not issuing notes, were brought together in the 1844 Bank Charter Act. Only banks already issuing notes could continue to do so, and the number of notes each could circulate was regulated. When banks amalgamated, the bank which was absorbed lost its note circulation, unless the new partnership had six persons or less. The long-term effect of this legislation was to reduce the number of banking partnerships in Britain, but by the expansion of branch-banking, the availability of banking facilities was progressively extended. The usefulness of sound banks showed clearly that the answer to early teething troubles lay not in a decline in the practice of banking, but in setting professional standards to make the business work as it should. The same policy applied to the notes the banks issued: despite their unpopularity in some quarters, bank notes remained an increasingly important form of currency, the laws regulating their issue simply serving to enhance their status. One result of these changes was an increase in the area of circulation of notes, and with this, in the need for good security printing.

Artists and engravers

Notes issued by country banks in the middle and late decades of the nineteenth century now seem sophisticated largely in relation to what had gone before. Stylistically they may be seen as a bridge between the paper money of the eighteenth century and that of the modern day, in that they took the traditional format, and transformed it with production techniques and design elements which hinted at things to come. This is not to say, however, that they did not have a clear identity of their own; on the contrary, the rich and romantic composition of their new design was entirely consonant with the mood of the Victorian age. Nineteenth-century notes exemplified the prevailing belief that art and commerce existed to serve each other, and the artists, engravers and printers who produced them were undoubtedly practising the craft of industrial design.

It is impossible to put an exact figure on the number of bank note printers and engravers there were. This is true of other branches of these arts and for the same reason, namely that there was relatively little specialisation and a lot of overlap between different fields. This applied to the medium with which people worked – for example, few engravers worked exclusively on either copper or steel – and the sort of work they undertook. James Fenton, an engraver in Dundee, describes himself on his letter-heading as an engraver and copper-plate and lithographic printer, able to produce a range of items including cards, invoices, circulars, funeral letters, coats of arms, cheques, and bank notes. This is typical, and quite a contrast with the situation today, when security-printing, like banking, is concentrated in the hands of a few major firms; and note engraving can be a highly-specialised, full-time job. In theory any printer or engraver listed in a nineteenth-century directory might have had occasion to work on bank notes. The best evidence comes from the notes themselves, which were often signed with the engraver's name, and sometimes his address, usually near the vignette or some other ornamental device, or at the bottom edge of the note. The British Museum collection of nineteenth-century British notes yields some sixty names; no doubt there were more, as many notes are unsigned, and the collection is by no means complete. It is, however, fairly representative, so we may use this as an approximate guide for comparison with other branches of engraving, and by these standards, producing bank notes was, even then, relatively specialised work.[4] It appears also, that there were degrees of specialisation within the field. Some names, such as F.Bartolozzi, an eminent engraver, appear on very few notes, suggesting that this was not a very large part of their output. At the other extreme the names of Silvester, Ashby, Lizars and Perkins are found on so many notes, from many different banks, as to suggest that bank notes must have been a regular and significant source of work. The large majority of bank note engravers were based in London. A few worked in the larger provincial cities, such as Newcastle, Leeds, Manchester, Liverpool, Birmingham and Bristol; as a rule their names are found on local notes, and generally in the first quarter of the century. Glasgow and Edinburgh were also significant centres for note engravers, especially for Scottish banks, although Lizars' firm in Edinburgh, taken over by W. & A.K.Johnston after Lizars' death in 1859, did work for over eighty banks throughout the British Isles.

The size of printing and engraving firms clearly varied a great deal. From the 1830s the growing popularity of illustrated books and cheap decorative prints offered new opportunities for work for engravers, and their numbers increased considerably. Some engravers, including Charles Heath and the Findens (who worked on bank notes), were able to support production

(Above, left)
Allegorical figure,
sailing ship and
ploughman in a
vignette engraved by
Livesey of Leeds for a
Thirsk Bank 5 guinea
note, 1809. (detail)
CM 1981—11—22—638.
(193 × 93 mm)

(Above right) A
graceful allegorical
figure framed by
traditional reeds, roses
and thistles on an
otherwise plain note
engraved by Perkins
and Bacon for a Bank
of Manchester £10 note
of 1839. (detail)
CM 1981—11—22—346.
(205 × 130 mm)

workshops with long-term employees, while printing firms took on more staff.[5] Others, like Charles Warren, continued to operate on a small scale, with only a few assistants or apprentices. On the evidence of bank notes, the quality of engraving was also variable, though not necessarily in any direct relation to the scale of operation: Perkins and Heath and Charles Warren both produced first-rate work though at opposite ends of the spectrum with regard to size. On the other hand, evidence presented to the 1836 Select Committee lamented that there were now too many would-be engravers, some sadly lacking in the important prerequisites of good taste and sound draughtsmanship.[6] Presumably then, bankers had a choice of engravers, and it may be that the less polished vignettes occur on notes of banks which chose cheaper and less able people. It is interesting, though, that variations in standard on the vignettes of even the larger firms' notes indicate that the quality of their engravers was far from consistent, particularly with regard to figure-drawing.

The designs on nineteenth-century bank notes are perhaps most remarkable for their variety. Allegorical figures, floral decorations, local features and topography, and abstract machine-engraved patterns were the most popular components, individually or in combination. As we shall see, the variety was made possible by contemporary developments in art and technology, and it is tempting to describe the period as one of steady progress towards increasingly

A charming scene of
cider-making on a £10
note of the Ross Bank,
Herefordshire, of the
1820s.
CM 1981–11–22–528.
(183 × 104 mm)

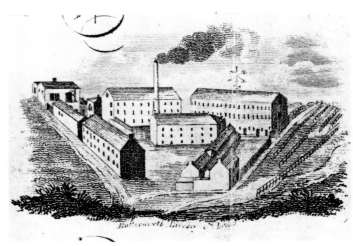

Town and country:
smoking factory
chimney on a £1 note
of the 1820s from
Dewsbury near Leeds,
and sheep-shearing on
a Whitby Bank £1
note of the early 1800s.
CM 1981–11–22–156.
(187 × 90 mm)
CM 1981–11–22–669.
(197 × 113 mm)

complex and modern notes. But that would be misleading, because part of the variety and interest of the nineteenth-century notes lies in the persistence of traditional ideas alongside the new. A ten pound note of the Brighthelmston Bank, issued in 1841, carries an allegorical female figure in a foliated cartouche very similar to that on Bank of England notes, and this closely derivative style, if uncommon, was not exceptional. Two notes from Yeovil Old Bank show a rather surprising reversion from a free and graceful vignette of Britannia in 1814 to a very much more stylised and formal figure in a cartouche on notes of the 1830s and 1840s. Probably it was the deliberate choice of the bankers to eschew the latest trends. There were, after all, plenty of engravers capable of producing more delicate and detailed work if it were wanted, and even they were sometimes called upon to produce very traditional designs. For example, notes issued by the Bank of Manchester in 1839 are plain in the manner of those of the Bank of England, adorned only with a graceful allegorical vignette in the top left-hand corner, yet they were engraved by Perkins and Bacon, renowned for their highly-decorative geometric machine-engraving. Devices or scenes of local significance were also a well-established source of embellishment which remained popular. One of the most distinctive and charming instances is a lively view of cider-making on a note of the Ross Bank, Herefordshire, in the 1820s, which is reminiscent of a medieval woodcut. However, the nineteenth-century vignettes are interesting not only for local colour, but because they reflect the sharpening contrast between industry and agriculture, town and country. Richard Silvester's bucolic sheep-shearing scene for Whitby Bank, early in the century, and the smoking factory chimneys engraved in the 1820s for a bank in Dewsbury, near Leeds, by the local firm of Butterworth & Company, are worlds apart.

Nonetheless, while acknowledging the continuation of familiar themes, it remains true that many bank notes in the nineteenth century broke away from the conventional mould, and demonstrate by their lavish graphic content both the artistic spirit of the age, and the practical belief in technology applied to art for the sake of commerce. This may be seen most clearly by focusing on the work of a few major nineteenth-century printers and engravers.

The most dramatic innovation came from technical developments in machine-engraving, producing kaleidoscopic abstract patterns which are the direct antecedents of the background security printing on modern bank notes. This work is primarily associated with Jacob Perkins, the American inventor who came to London to offer his designs to the Bank of England and patented his method for case-hardening steel-plates so that an infinite number of printing-plates could be produced from one master-plate.[7] This paved the way for other types of steel-engraving, book illustration for example, but printing from steel offered two potential advantages for bank notes. Firstly, although

the initial costs of the metal and the engraving would be higher,[8] steel should in the long run be cheaper than copper plates, which had to be frequently replaced. Secondly, steel offered greater security because having just one master plate should ensure that every note was absolutely identical, removing the risk of slight variations in newly-engraved plates, however carefully they were done. This promise of exact reproduction encouraged the use of the geometric lathe to engrave patterns of such precision and intricacy that they could scarcely be repeated even by machine.

Perkins had developed his siderography, or exact transfer process for steel plates, in America. It was taken up there by Gideon Fairman, a partner in a firm which switched from book-plates to the more lucrative job of printing bank notes in the mid 1810s. Another colleague, Asa Spencer, developed the art of engraving complex patterns by rose-engine, or geometric lathe. The lathe operated with a large number of cogs and wheels of varying sizes and toothed edges, which could be arranged in many different combinations to produce an enormous number of permutations of pattern. In 1819, Perkins and Fairman offered a combined package to the Bank of England. That cautious institution doubted the practicality of their methods, but there was plenty of support elsewhere. Thomas Bewick, himself a pace-setter in the craft of wood-cut, thought Perkins' engine-turning 'beautiful,' and believed his designs to be 'inimitable and quite sufficient to answer the end intended.'[9]

Specimen £5 note for the North Wilts Banking Company, Melksham Branch, by Skipper & East, incorporating the varieties of machine engraving recommended in the 1844 Bankers' Magazine. CM 1981–11–22–680. (204 × 123 mm)

Specimen £1 note for
the Leeds Union Bank,
engraved by Perkins
and Heath with their
distinctive blend of
classical allegory and
geometric machine
engraving.
CM 1981−11−22−282.
(169 × 91 mm)

Scotia in a tartan
plaid resting on a cliff
top on a specimen £1
note by Perkins, Bacon
& Co. for the North of
Scotland Banking
Company c.1850.
(detail)
CM 1985−9−20−2.
(159 × 121 mm)

Many bankers obviously thought so too, because Perkins and Fairman, now
joined by Charles Heath, one of the foremost British engravers, are among
the names most frequently seen on provincial bank notes. Their style is
distinctive: traditional allegorical figures and coats of arms surrounded by
the dense ornament of machine-engraved borders and medallions. If in 1826
Charles Heath had to sell off stock engravings to make up for business lost
because of banks failing in the 1825/1826 crisis,[10] this only shows how
important their bank work was; and indeed, it did not slump for long, for
with various changes in partnership, the firm continued to print notes for

A demure
personification of
Justice framed in an oval
machine-engraved
border for a Bradford
Old Bank £20 note
produced by Perkins,
Fairman and Heath.
(detail)
CM 1980–11–30–46.
(195 × 107 mm)

Mercury engraved
by Gideon Fairman on a
£20 proof note of Jones
Loyd's Manchester
Bank. (detail)
CM 1981–11–22–347.
(192 × 100 mm)

Allegorical figures
representing Hibernia,
Britannia and Scotia
canopied by dancing
cherubs and flower
garland on a Saddle-
worth Union Bank
£1 note of 1825. (detail).
CM 1980—11—30—318.
(185 × 100 mm)

banks in Britain, and indeed all over the world, until into the twentieth
century.

It may be mentioned here that steel-plates were not always accompanied
by complex engine-engraving: banks in Ludlow and Halifax in the 1820s had
notes engraved on steel which are really quite plain. However several other
firms followed Perkins' line. For example, in 1844 the first volume of the
Bankers' Magazine devoted an article to the dangers of forgery, and included
samples of different kinds of machine-engraving by another important security
printer, Charles Skipper and East, demonstrating 'fixed patterns' which
relied on evenness and precision for security, and 'random' or 'eccentric'
patterns, produced by 'accidental' settings of the machine, which, it was
claimed, would be impossible to reproduce.[11] These devices were very similar
to Perkins' engine-engraving, particularly the panel repeating the value of
the note in words composed of tiny letters.

In contrast to earlier practice, when notes relied predominantly upon simple
script or a small ornamental device for security, from the 1820s bankers
began to heed the recommendation that they combine several different
talents in the production of their notes. The brilliant but rather impersonal
geometric machine-engraving was, therefore, often accompanied by softer
hand-engraved vignettes, which, in style and subject matter, drew heavily
on current fashion. The work of the Edinburgh engraver and printer, W.H.
Lizars, shows clearly how in this respect bank note design reflected the
broader influences of contemporary taste.

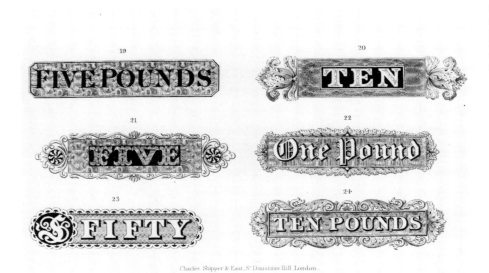

Skipper & East's designs for a sum piece, using fixed and random patterns, ornamental lettering, and acanthus leaves.

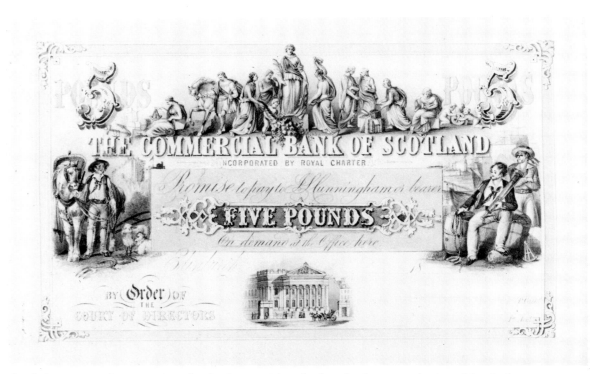

Sketch for a £5 note by W.H. Lizars for the Commercial Bank of Scotland, *c.* 1850, dominated by the frieze on the façade of the new head office building. CM. 1980–3–58–2. (229 × 142 mm)

One of the most pervasive of these influences was neo-classicism. This dated back to the artistic revival of the eighteenth century, which witnessed a shift of mood away from rococo flamboyance to what was seen as the formality of art in antiquity. Many believed that 'the imitation of the ancients is the only way of excelling in the sublime and elegant arts of Painting and Sculpture';[12] classical subjects were therefore an important part of the curricula of the new art schools and institutions, and as such they influenced the talents of pupils who became the professional artists of a later age. Lizars studied at the Trustees Academy in Edinburgh, which, having been founded in c.1760, was one of the earliest art schools. Initially the Academy had concentrated on mechanical arts, such as damask weaving, but by the time Lizars attended, between 1802 and 1805, it had become a school of design, and had for that purpose formed 'a fine collection of casts from the choicest examples of the antique.'[13]

The pursuit of the purity and excellence which seemed to be embodied in classical forms was as much a matter of principle as of practice.[14] However sordid the reality of industrialisation might sometimes be, it was nonetheless often motivated by high ideals of human endeavour. This was as true of banking as of any other developing business. Although many banks foundered

Allegorical figures representing Britannia and Plenty, with fruit tumbling from her cornucopia, engraved by Lizars for a £50 note of the Leeds & West Riding Banking Company. (detail) CM 1981–11–22–298. (223 × 139 mm)

in the commercial crises of the nineteenth century, most aspired to standards of wealth and security symbolised by the classical figures which appeared in their architecture and on their notes. A note design engraved by Lizars for the Commercial Bank of Scotland around 1850 is dominated by the frieze of allegorical figures on the pediment of the Bank's head office building, the full façade of which appears in a small vignette at the foot of the note.

It is clear, however, that on bank notes as elsewhere, classical motifs were not taken directly from prototypes in the ancient world. They were unashamedly neo-classical, translating the ancient forms and later imitations into a contem-

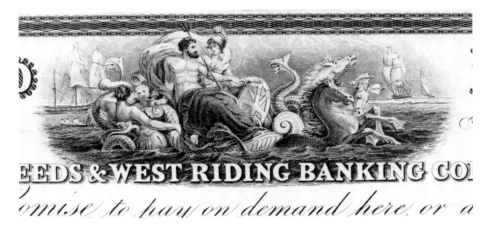

(Above) Lizars' vignette of Britannia ruling the waves with Neptune on a £10 note for the Leeds & West Riding Banking Company. (detail) CM 1981−11−22−297. (187 × 110 mm)

Pen and wash sketch of the coat of arms used on Lizars' designs for the Leeds Bank. CM 1981−11−22−285. (32 × 37 mm)

Mask of Medusa
in machine-ruled
medallions contrasting
with soft roses, from a
£5 proof design of the
Huddersfield Banking
Company. (detail)
CM 1981—11—22—244.
(195 × 100 mm)

Neo-classical
romance in Lizars'
dreamy Apollo framed
by honeysuckle,
acanthus, and olive
branches. Detail from a
design probably for the
York Union Banking
Company.
CM 1981—11—22—459.
(201 × 117 mm)

porary idiom. The allegorical figures on Lizars' bank notes illustrate this perfectly, combining the rather formal grace of classicism with the freedom of nineteenth-century romanticism. Agriculture and industry, primary sources of wealth whose needs brought banks into existence, were personified by elegant figures surrounded by sheaves of corn or scientific instruments, while nymphs representing Justice and Plenty conveyed banks' promises of fair dealing and financial good fortune. The most popular figure was Britannia, who appeared armed with plumed helmet, shield and trident as the leading character in a variety of dramatic scenes. In a particularly exuberant design for the Leeds and West Riding Banking Company she is seated next to Neptune, her cloak billowing behind her as she rules the waves from a chariot drawn by plunging sea-horses. More often she is placed against a background of city skylines, factory chimneys, or the harbours and sea trade so fundamental to Britain's economic prosperity.

In addition to these symbolic figures, Lizars and many other note engravers made liberal use of motifs from classical ornament. In exotic displays of naturalistic and stylised foliage, full-blown roses and jagged thistles bloom among cornucopiae overflowing with fruits. Even quite simple notes were likely to have decorative borders or medallions punctuated at the corners with an anthemion or honeysuckle pattern. Acanthus leaves were everywhere; the backs of notes were often smothered with floral scrolls and curling acanthus leaves. A design almost certainly engraved for the York Union

without Stamp Pr Act 9 Geo. IV

(Top) A Lincoln street full of activity with the
cathedral in the distance on a specimen £5 note by
Lizars for the Hull Banking Company, Lincoln
branch. (detail). CM 1981–11–22–311.
(218 × 135 mm)

(Above) A view of Inverness by Lizars used on
the Caledonian Banking Company £1 note between
1833 and 1863. (detail). CM 1981–11–9–65.
(167 × 133 mm)

(Right) An attractive vignette of the Royal
Pavilion is an appropriate subject for a Brighton
Royal Bank £1 note of 1823. CM 1980–11–30–48.
(194 × 104 mm)

Banking Company shows most clearly the neo-classical influence, portraying Apollo cloud-borne in a circlet of honeysuckle and acanthus.

The second contemporary trend in art which was adapted for bank notes was that of landscape painting and topographical views. This was also bound up with developments in printing, for the use of steel-engraving to mass-produce pictures as prints created a market for reasonably inexpensive illustrated books, and romantic landscapes were a popular subject. Turner, for example, used the recently-improved medium of watercolour to paint landscapes which were then engraved for publication in books and journals. As for many other engravers, book illustrations accounted for a large part of W.H. Lizars' output. The subjects varied from anatomical plates for medical textbooks written by one of his younger brothers, to etchings for Audubon's *Birds of America*, but architectural and topographical studies predominate. In 1818, for example, he collaborated with Turner and Walter Scott on a volume of *Provincial Antiquities and Picturesque Scenery of Scotland*.

On a smaller scale, views like this were appropriate for country banks: fine engravings of local landmarks would appeal to local pride, and the hardness of steel-plates offered the benefit of sharper detail and subtle shading to challenge potential counterfeiters. Lizars' views on bank notes ranged in theme from a panorama of Perth to a bustling street in Lincoln, and from the natural beauty of the Lake District to the architectural splendour of York Minster. All convey almost tangible qualities of light and atmosphere, and it is perhaps in these miniature scenes that popular taste, the skill of an artist and engraver, and the bankers' need for security, were most effectively combined.

Clyde shipping engraved by Joseph Swan of Glasgow for a Greenock Bank Company specimen £1 note, bordered by a frieze of little ships. (detail)
CM 1981–11–9–147.
(190 × 122 mm)

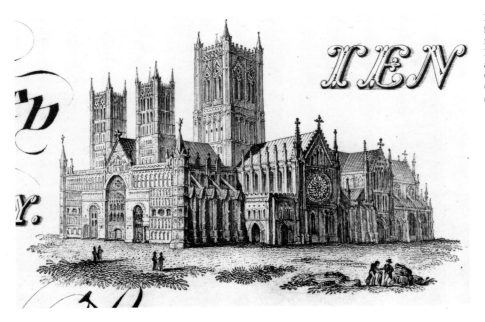

Lincoln Cathedral from a specimen £10 note by Perkins and Bacon for the Lincoln and Lindsey Banking Company. (detail) CM 1981—11—22—320. (189 × 101 mm)

Art and technology each contributed in their own ways to the security of bank notes, but they were not alternatives: neither offered sufficient protection on its own. The need to combine different skills in one design had been emphasised repeatedly in the Society of Arts report in 1819, and engraving firms like Perkins and Lizars endorsed their proposal. Perkins, essentially a scientist, employed top engravers like Charles Heath and William Holl to engrave elegant vignettes for his notes, while Lizars, by choice an artist, experimented with new engraving methods and made extravagant use of abstract machine-engraving. However, the matter was still being debated in the middle of the nineteenth century, kept alive no doubt by the continuing incidence of forgery, and the Bank of England's determined adherence to a simple black and white note embellished only by the Britannia medallion. The Bank believed that years of familiarity with an unchanging design would train the public to spot a forgery, and it is interesting that some of the most successful and long-lived provincial banks also had very simple notes, exhibiting few alterations in design. Several critics, however, pointed out that to be effective, even a familiar image must be excellently executed. In 1844 the *Bankers' Magazine* dismissed the Bank of England Britannia as 'a ludicrous and wretched affair', and pointed in contrast to the allegorical vignettes on country notes, and postage stamps, on which 'the engraving of the Queen's head on the engine work has been found sufficient to defy any attempt at imitation.'[15] In 1856, the year after the Bank of England introduced a new, but utterly conventional five pound note, the cause was taken up in a lecture given by Henry Bradbury to the Royal Institution in London.[16]

Portraits of Queen
Victoria and Prince
Albert from a proof
£20 note engraved by
W.H. Lizars for the
Commercial Bank of
Scotland c.1850.
(detail)
CM 1982—9—25—4.
(217 × 135 mm)

Bradbury was a partner in the new security printing firm of Bradbury and
Evans, and he followed the contemporary faith in art and science combined:
'The union of Art, in which our country has been deficient, with Manufacture
in which she is unrivalled . . ., would place England in advance of every
other nation.'[17] To illustrate his proposals, Bradbury had produced two
designs for a 'simple' and 'complex' note, each with engravings by the artist
John Leighton.

The simple note relied upon art for security, with a striking Britannia and
capital letters entwined with realistic rose stems. The role of art was 'to stamp
upon the production an *individuality*, expressing qualities which are not
within the province of Mechanical imitation. The work which has the genius
of an artist imprinted upon it, is not to be imitated by an inferior mind . . .'[18]
Bradbury recommended intaglio engraving, because 'Possessing the greatest
delicacy of details, greatest power of light and shade, it is the only process
capable of giving the combination of purity and power which distinguishes
the true fine-Art production.'[19]

The complex note retained many of the same decorative elements, but
placed them against a background of dense machine-engraving. Henry Brad-

bury summed up clearly the problem of whether detailed machine-work made forgeries easier or harder to detect:

Too much ornamentation is apt to bewilder, nay misguide – too little is apt to abuse: but a proper combination of elaborate mechanical work, properly balanced to meet the effect of the design, will also combine beauty with security, with hardly less facility of recognition.[20]

Experimenting with colour

In the first two decades of the century, some provincial banks had begun to print the back of their notes, or some element of the face of their notes, in colour; this may perhaps reflect the taste for Gothic art and medieval manuscripts, with their illuminated initial letters or borders. However the use of colour on notes was limited, and even by the end of the century, it was by no means a major feature of bank notes.

Although the mechanisation of colour printing occurred relatively slowly, by the middle of the century cheap colour prints were available. The demand for colour printing – a natural development from the demand for prints generally – was satisfied by the greater availability of coloured inks, which had been harder to make and more expensive than black ink, and in the 1840s theatre posters were printed in combinations of two or three colours. It does appear, though, that colour was still reserved for specialised kinds of printing: T.C.Hansard reported in 1841 that colour was usually applied to pictorial fine-art reproductions, and was seldom used for run-of-the-mill printing jobs.[21] Bank notes probably fell into the latter category.

In the middle of the century both theoretical and practical interest in colour on bank notes was stimulated by concern to prevent forgery by the rapidly improving science of photography. A.Claudet wrote a letter in *The Times*, explaining that he had informed M.Marshall, the Chief Cashier of the Bank of England, that in photographic experiments he had managed to reproduce the watermarks on the Bank's notes. To prevent fraud he suggested coloured inks, which at that time could not be reproduced photographically:

In photography, red, orange, yellow and green, produce black, while blue, indigo, and violet, produce white. Now, from these different properties of the various colours, it is evident that a Bank Note, with its printing, emblems, devices, writing, &c., printed in variegated colours, would offer the greatest difficulties to the perpetration of the fraud; for the lightest colours to the eye would produce the darkest effect in the copy, while the darkest colours, such as blue, indigo and violet, would be hardly represented at all, or but very slightly. . . .

The Bank of England, and Bankers in general, instead of issuing notes in their present dull state of black and white, have only to transform them into the most elegant and ornamental coloured designs, and they will not only frustrate all attempts of the forger, but have the advantage of enlivening the serious appearance of their counters, and spread an artistic taste among the mercantile community.[22]

It took the Bank of England almost eighty years to follow Claudet's advice, but 'bankers in general' were a little more adventurous. For the most part, colour printing on English provincial bank notes in the second half of the century (if it were used at all) was still restricted to a part of the design: often an overlay of the note's value in words, or printing in one colour on the back of the note. There are elaborate coloured proofs of designs by Lizars; for example, blue machine-engraved borders and medallions for the Whitehaven Joint Stock Bank, and a stunning design for the Bradford Joint Stock Commercial Bank with an orange vignette and machine border surrounded by a blue baroque floral scroll. These show a willingness to experiment with more sophisticated colour printing, but it is very uncertain that they were ever adopted.[23]

Difficulties in developing methods of colour intaglio and lithographic printing may have been a constraint, as intaglio, especially, was an important process in bank note printing. Nevertheless, in the 1850s and 1860s several major banks in Scotland took up colour printing, often using lithography. The Royal Bank of Scotland was clearly aware of the risks of photography; they attempted to reproduce by this means a five pound note of 1856 of quite a plain style to which had been added by hand a slim panel of green oak leaves, and the words 'FIVE POUNDS' in red, both across the main text. The resulting reproduction renders all aspects – black, green and red – in a faint sepia tone. This design was not adopted; however in 1860 the Bank produced a one pound note in blue, and in the following year, W. & A. K. Johnston printed a note in black with a red lithographic overlay. This practice was followed by the Bank of Scotland, the British Linen Company, the Commercial Bank of Scotland, the National Bank and the Union Bank, all of which had their notes printed by Perkins Bacon in black or blue with a coloured overprint, usually red. Again, the overprint was generally produced by lithography, a method of printing from a flat surface, by making use of the principle that water and grease repel each other. The areas to be printed are drawn with a greasy substance, and the rest of the surface dampened with water. The greasy printing ink is then attracted to the greasy drawn areas, but repelled by the water on the rest of the surface.[24] Lithography was invented in Munich in the late 1790s, and, during the nineteenth century, developed as an important medium for commercial printing in Britain. That Perkins' firm, which had encouraged other experimental branches of printing, should also have adopted this method was appropriate; it also pointed the way for the future, as modern notes are produced with a combination of lithography, and detailed intaglio engravings.

Art and commerce

The graphic design of nineteenth-century bank notes mirrored the broad contemporary attitude to the role of art. By the 1830s the government was concerned that Britain was lagging behind the continent in the application of art to commercial manufactures, and a select committee was appointed to look into ways 'of extending a knowledge of the Arts and of the Principles of Design among the People [especially the manufacturing Population] of the Country . . .'[25] The Committee's Report of 1836 found that the provision for art education was inadequate to meet the degree of interest in the arts, and led to Government-sponsored schools of design.

The effectiveness of these efforts was evidently open to debate, for while few disapproved of encouraging public appreciation of art, there were those who worried about the public's taste, and what exactly it might appreciate. In 1816 the Edinburgh Annual Register reviewed the current state of the Arts of Design in Britain, and reported rather disapprovingly that:

The taste for historical works and heroic landscape now no longer exists, and the talents of our engravers have for a long time been directed to topographical subjects, architectural antiquities, vignettes and other book decorations, which although they have tended little to improve the taste or extend the boundaries of art, have at least displayed much beautiful execution.[26]

By 1840 art galleries, print shops, and the popular illustrated annuals made art more accessible than ever, but critics still deprecated the taste of the majority of the British public. Thus Thackeray contemptuously describing the contents of a typical illustrated album: 'Flowers, Gems, Souvenirs, Caskets of Loveliness, Beauty, as they may be called; glaring caricatures of flowers, singly, in groups, in flower-pots, or with horrid, deformed little Cupids sporting among them . . .'[27]

Topographical subjects, vignettes, flowers and even cupids – they all featured on the bank notes of the time. No doubt then, these were not examples of great Art, but if the currency reflected broad public taste, was that any bad thing? And as the Edinburgh Annual Register had remarked of the engraving profession as a whole, many of the notes showed beautiful craftsmanship. By looking at just one aspect of many vignettes – the sky – we can see that engravers approached bank work with no less care than they would a larger, commercial print. A contemporary writer explained the technique for engraving sky:

A serene sky is represented by strokes parallel to the horizon, or by strokes following the same direction, but gently waved. According to the general rule for the sky, the strokes must be gradually stronger as they recede from the horizon.[28]

Evidently this was not an easy task. The Great Exhibition of 1851 included a steel-plate engraved with a machine-ruled sky, described in the catalogue as 'perhaps the most severe test to which a steel plate can be subjected.' The

(Above) Roses, thistles and clover entwined on a £5 note for the Lincoln and Lindsey Banking Company, c.1862. (detail)
CM 1981–11–22–318.
(193 × 103 mm)

(Above right) Detail from a £5 proof for the Halifax and Huddersfield Union Bank reveals a cherub nestling in a figure '5' formed of acanthus leaves.
CM 1981–11–22–219.
(191 × 121 mm)

landscape views on bank notes – often engraved from steel plates – show just the same technique, with effective results.

In the field of geometric lathe work, bank notes were innovators rather than followers of fashion, at least with regard to the method of production. The ornamental effect of the patterns does have a rather curious contemporary counterpart, for the intricately interlocking lines bear a close resemblance to the lace patterns for ceremonial embroidery, as used for example on nineteenth-century regimental uniforms.[29] But as a style and technique of engraving, the complex machine work introduced early in the century was perhaps the first element of note design to become an important form of security printing in its own right. The richly decorative notes engraved by Perkins and Waterlow for several Scottish banks at the end of the nineteenth and the opening of the twentieth centuries show how this skill had developed: one writer praised the 'exquisite' lathe engravings, because they 'approach more closely to nature's works than almost any kind of artistic effect – the more they are magnified, the more perfect they appear.'[30]

As the graphic content of notes increased, surrounding hand-engraved vignettes with machine-engraved borders, and as more notes were printed on the back, and using colour, so the bank notes of Victorian Britain gave a promise of things to come in the multi-faceted production of twentieth-century notes. But in the style of their graphic design – limpid allegorical personifications and vignettes of city and country life, framed by dense geometric or floral ornament – these notes clearly proclaim that they are products of their age.

Bees symbolising industry and cottage-garden flowers from a Halifax and Huddersfield Union Bank £5 note by Rowe, Kentish and Co. The same vignette appeared on other notes by different engravers. (detail) CM 1981−11−22−219. (191 × 121 mm)

The rectangular proportions of the animal on a £10 note of the Burnley branch of the Craven Bank are typical of the art of the period. (detail) CM 1981−11−22−119. (187 × 112 mm)

An idyllic view of
hay-making on a £5
proof note by Lizars
for the Howden Branch
of the York City and
County Banking
Company.
CM 1981−11−22−236.
(229 × 139 mm)

A mysterious
encounter with a
cowled figure amongst
the ruins on a proof
£5 note of the Kendal
Bank.
CM 1981−11−22−438.
(200 × 120 mm)

Tradition at the Bank

The Bank had been under public scrutiny for virtually the whole of the Restriction period. It had been unjustly vilified for, as its critics saw it, helping to condemn to death relatively harmless people involved in passing forged notes; but in reality it was the severity of the penal code which was at fault and needed amending. (At that time more than two hundred offences were punishable with death.) Moreover those critics chose to ignore the compassion it had demonstrated in giving financial help to the families of those convicted, and the money given in some cases to convicts themselves so that they would not be penniless during the long voyage to Botany Bay. They also forgot that an utterer of notes – and this was a capital offence – was often allowed to plead guilty to the lesser offence of possession which carried the penalty of transportation; but then when the question was raised of whether the Royal Prerogative was being compromised there was much tut-tutting and the Bank's corporate knuckles were rapped.

It is not surprising then, that when the Restriction ended together with the issue of one and two pound notes, the Bank sighed with relief and retired thankfully from the limelight seemingly choosing, as far as the design of its notes was concerned, to return to the status quo. But the spectre of small notes had not finished with the Bank and it reappeared towards the end of 1825. A speculative boom which began in 1824 had, by the spring of the following year, gained sufficient momentum to cause concern in official circles.[31] The boom had been fuelled by the flotation of several hundred 'bubble' type companies financed in the absence of the Bank's small notes, by those of the country banks which, as a result, were dangerously over-extended. The preferred practice of the country banks when payment of one of their notes was demanded was to exchange it for a Bank of England note as they had done during the Restriction period;[32] but trouble began brewing for them once the outcome of a Parliamentary debate, resulting from the refusal of a provincial bank to pay one of its notes in gold, had been publicised.[33] The bank in question had no right to refuse as many people realised for the first time. Matters came to a head in December and the Bank consulted the Government: gold reserves were low and the situation as dangerous as in 1797, but this time there was no question of a return to the Restriction.[34]

There were several ways in which the Bank helped to restore public confidence and credit and conserve its coin, but we shall only concern ourselves with one. It was the issue of approximately one million one pound notes which had been printed during the Restriction but never used.[35] These notes quickly went to the provinces where this time they were welcomed and satisfied those who had previously only been content with coin. Perhaps it was to be expected that forgery would raise its ugly head and those who thought so were not disappointed. The number of forged one pound notes presented at the Bank both in 1826 (1601) and in 1827 (1695) was virtually triple the figure for the previous year (579) whilst prosecutions leapt from four in 1825 to twenty-three in 1826 and thirty-eight in the following year; further proof, if indeed any was needed, that the smaller denominations were attractive to the forgers.[36] Once the crisis was over and the country banks had been culled – some thirty-seven issuers had gone to the wall – the recriminations began;[37] the Bank blamed the country banks and the country banks blamed the Bank. It was true that the Bank had been guilty of sitting on its hands; for a while anyway, in tune with public opinion which held that those who indulged in the rash speculation that initiated the whole series of events should bear the consequences. But the seat of the problem was fundamental and irrefutable: it lay with the irresponsible expansion of so many small independent note issues. Cobbett put it well in *Rural Rides*:

The Bank is blamed for putting out paper and causing high prices; and blamed at the same time for not putting out paper to accommodate merchants and keep them from breaking. It cannot be to blame for both, and indeed it is blamable for neither. It is the fellows that put out the paper and then break that do the mischief.[38]

When the dust had settled Parliament decided that no bank should issue notes for less than five pounds (they could never have guessed that almost 120 years later this would be the Bank of England's highest denomination) and that note-issuing joint-stock banks should be allowed, but only outside the sixty-five mile radius of London.[39] Almost by way of a concession to the Bank because of this diminution of its monopolistic position established by the 1708 Act, it was allowed to establish branches and issue its notes, payable at the provincial location or in London. These proved to be excellent bridge-heads from which to compete with and even, in the case of the more combative, to challenge the provincial note-issuers who were offered preferential rates of discount if they would renounce their rights of issue and handle the Bank's notes instead.

Before turning once more to note design and production let us continue to look at and consider the impact of contemporary legislation on the Bank's note issue. Whilst the 1826 Act had permitted the establishment of note-issuing joint-stock banks operating outside London there was some confusion about whether these banks could open offices in London for other banking business. An Act passed in 1833[40] clarified the position and joint-stock banks opened in London; this had been the ultimate goal of Thomas Joplin who had crusaded since 1822 for the joint-stock system, holding up the Scottish banks as a good example of stable banking. (When, in preparation for the 1826 Act, it was proposed to prohibit small notes in Scotland as well for uniformity's sake, it caused an uproar and even Sir Walter Scott reached for his pen. Justifiably he wrote 'We are well, our pulse and complexion prove it – let those who are sick take physic.') The 1833 Act also recognised the Bank's notes and made them legal tender for all amounts above five pounds. This meant that in the event of a crisis similar to the one in 1825 as long as the credit of the Bank itself remained good, the public would be satisfied with its notes and its reserves would consequently be safeguarded.

The Bank Charter Act of 1844[41] was a watershed in the Bank's history; amongst the provisions of the Act, the issue of notes was to be kept entirely separate from the Bank's commercial business; it was legally obliged to buy bar gold at £3–17–9 a standard ounce and to pay its notes in sovereigns.[42] This of course meant that for the first time in England and Wales the gold standard operated on a legal basis. There were to be no new issuers of notes and those whose issues lapsed forfeited their right to issue. In short the Act considerably fortified the Bank's position and the standing of its note issue in England and Wales.

` Moving on to note design and production, the remaining banks of issue had been able to draw on the fund of expertise accumulated during the search for inimitability, and superb examples of security printing were developed in which art and technology combined, a policy which had been so often recommended to the Bank. As has been already mentioned, the Deputy Governor had returned from a visit to the Bank of Ireland in 1832 enthusing about their printing methods.[43] Consequently J.S.Bawtree and his assistant were sent to Dublin to inspect the plant and report back. The Bank of Ireland's system was well in advance of the Bank's; the presses were steam-driven; the method of dampening the paper was simple and yet more effective than the Bank's; steam was used for warming the plates and drying the notes but it was the method of numbering which particularly impressed Bawtree and his assistant, because the constant moving-on by hand required with the

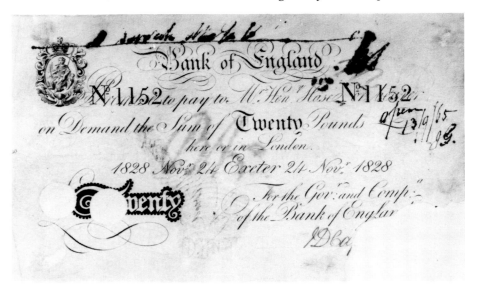

The 1826 Country Bankers Act allowed the Bank to establish branches in the provinces. The only known surviving note issued by the short-lived (1827–34) Exeter branch. (205 × 127 mm)

108

£5 note dated
1 May 1838.
Plate-printed by
the new methods
introduced by the
ex-Bank of Ireland
employee, John
Oldham.
(210 × 125 mm)

machines at the Bank was unnecessary with the Irish method. It had been invented by John Oldham, their Engineer and Chief Engraver, and numbered notes '. . .1, . . .2' in almost the same fashion as today. (Bramah's method was '1 . . ., 2 . . .' which for technical reasons involved moving the units wheel by hand.) The system also included a Plate Transfer Press and this, as we know, was the route to achieving 'identity' or sameness of issue.

The outcome of the investigation was that after negotiations with the Bank of Ireland, John Oldham moved to England in 1836 and was appointed 'Mechanical Engineer and Principal of the Engraving, Plate Printing, Numbering and Dating Office' and supervised the installation of the new machinery in the Bank.[44] Later that year when Oldham's system came into production the Bank achieved identity in its notes for the first time.

The time was now ripe for the Bank to consider redesigning its notes: the printing technology had been provided; all that was needed was a design combining several different methods of engraving and the result must surely be the ultimate in bank note production. A committee consisting of the Governor, Deputy Governor and four Directors met for the first time in September 1838 when the Governor told them that he had sought the advice of a distinguished painter, Henry Corbould, a first-rate line-engraver, Henry LeKeux, and the Royal Mint's designer, William Wyon, about the new note.[45] The Committee approved an outline design for the proposed note sketched by Corbould; it was to incorporate historical, script, machine, stipple and medallion engraving.[46] A sub-committee was then formed of expert advisers including, of course, the three experts consulted by the Governor, plus the celebrated engraver J.H.Robinson, C.R.Cockerell, the Bank's architect and John Oldham. The result was an extravagant design

Preliminary sketch for the Committee-designed note proposed in 1838 but not adopted. It was dismissed by one of the Bank's Directors as 'a picture with a note in the middle'.

bearing the promissory clause in the centre between two standing Britannias (the minute records that it was based on a statue of Juno 'at the RA')[47] whilst a vignette of William and Mary in profile (the work of Wyon using 'medallion engraving')[48] was supported by Mercury and Fortune (the former being the god of commerce is often portrayed together with his staff of office or caduceus in connection with banking).

The Court of Directors did not care for it, however; they felt that they should have been presented with more than just one design. Why not invite artists of the calibre of Chantrey, Callcott and Westmacott? Probably the most damning comment was that it resembed 'a picture with a note in the middle'[49] and when compared with the style of the Bank's notes − until then a note first and foremost with the occasional minor concession to art − it is difficult not to agree. Of course, in the end the question comes down to one of priorities: was the Bank's first priority to produce a simple note that was unforgeable, or an artistic note that was unforgeable? If at all possible the former was the preferred option for two reasons: throughout the search for the inimitable note the Bank's unerring policy had been to prefer simplicity. It was, the Special Committee had contended, easier to forge a complex note than a simple one. The other reason for the rejection of the expert's work was the Bank's innate conservatism. Whether this proposed combination of the arts would have confounded the forger we shall never know for the project was eventually shelved in 1842;[50] but harking back to the 1802 Special Committee again it is interesting to speculate how accurate a copy could have been made on copper by an averagely-competent engraver, and would it, had there been some reversal of roles, have been good enough to satisfy the original Special Committee?

In December 1854 the *London Gazette*[51] reported that all Bank of England notes dated 1 January 1855 and after would be of a new design. The Bank's Printing Department had been working since 1842 to produce a note that was as technically advanced as possible: although the printing technique used for the new note was criticised by some members of the printing fraternity, in the main the public reaction was favourable. *The Times* observed (on 11 January 1855) that 'Its appearance at a hasty glance is very little different from that of the old Note, although upon examination its superiority is very striking, both as regards clearness of execution of the design and the watermark of the paper'. It was a design that was to remain in circulation with but little change for over a hundred years.

The fundamental difference between the 1855 note and its predecessors lay in the method of printing: the new notes were produced by letterpress printing from electrotypes[52] whilst the old had, of course, been plate printed. There were several features which distinguished the new note from its predecessors: the quality of printing was improved; it bore a new specially-designed Britannia; it was, for the first time, payable 'to bearer' only; and it had a shaded watermark. The new Britannia had been commissioned, for a fee of £100, from Daniel Maclise. Britannia was depicted, full face, sitting

Matthew Marshall.
Chief Cashier of the
Bank 1835–64.
From an oil painting by
T. Mackinlay.

111

In 1855 a new design of Bank of England note surface printed from electrotypes was introduced. The Chief Cashier's name no longer appeared in the payee clause.
(217 × 128 mm)

holding a spear and dressed as a Saxon princess in an unmistakably pre-Raphaelite style. This delightful vignette appeared on every Bank of England note from 1855 – including the coloured series A introduced in 1928 – until 1957 and must certainly be one of the most frequently reproduced designs ever.

The second of the material changes concerned the removal of the Chief Cashier's name from the promissory clause. As we know the practice had begun soon after 1700 when the name of someone known to the Bank (generally simply a cashier) had been inserted before 'or Bearer' for legal reasons.[53] Nearly a hundred years later the name used was that of the Chief Cashier and it was being printed, but as by 1855 it had ceased to have any real significance the opportunity was taken with the introduction of the new notes to drop it. The signature on the note remained that of one of the cashiers; it had been printed from 1853 but the signature of the Chief Cashier was not finally to replace it until 1870.

Perhaps the most important feature of the new issue concerned the watermark. Seventeen years before, the Governor had criticised the watermark then being used – waved lines with the denomination in words – which was, he felt too easily forged.[54] William Brewer, the Bank's watermark mould-maker, eventually succeeded in producing a watermark with degrees of shading and this new development was taken up enthusiastically by the Bank who acquired the sole right to the invention and thus built into the note issue another important anti-forgery device.

Parts of the printing community, however, were unhappy about the change in printing methods and their cause was championed by Henry

Bradbury in his lecture at the Royal Institution in 1856.[55] He was in favour of printing by engraved plates using ornamental machine-engraving, and he was scathing in his criticism of the new notes which he suggested were 'unworthy of the Bank and of the Nation'; the only protection against forgery now lay, he thought, in the use of 'highly expensive paper'. In retrospect and bearing in mind that machine-engraving was eventually introduced it seems that he might have been right on that point but in other areas his argument was fallacious; the criticism he had of the new notes could equally be applied to the notes he proposed.

During the latter half of the nineteenth century the Bank had, on the whole, led a quiet, comfortable existence. There had been several heart-stopping events – the crash of Overend, Gurney in 1866 and the Baring crisis in 1890 to name the more familiar – but all had been contained. Nothing had occurred to shake the Bank's quiet confidence nurtured, no doubt, by the prestige and influence the nation was enjoying abroad. The Bank's notes were accepted world-wide, the forgery problem had considerably diminished since the 1820s and there seemed little or nothing to be gained by costly design change. As the summer of 1914 approached the old order was about to be changed and, as we shall discover, as far as the Bank's notes were concerned, things would never be quite the same again.

The 1855 design incorporated a Britannia designed by Daniel Maclise, RA. Detail from an issued bank note.

4 In pursuit of perfection

'Perfection is the child of time'[1]

In 1914 when rumblings from the Continent warned of the impending conflict they also signalled the demise of the old order. Very little throughout the world was to be unaffected by the chain of events which began in the Balkans. For the Bank's part, as far as its notes were concerned, it was to lead to another issuer coming on the scene, the use of colour-printing and to a sequence of events culminating in 1931 when its notes would no longer be literally 'as good as gold'.

Once the inevitability of war became apparent, plans began to be laid: as with the Restriction period more than a century before, the Government's aim was to safeguard the nation's gold resources for the war effort, some of which were represented by the gold sovereigns and half-sovereigns in the hands of the public. How might these coins be conserved so as to supplement official stocks for central government use? The solution was simple and obvious: it was to issue notes for one pound and ten shillings to supplant them. However, it was not to be a Bank of England issue. Several meetings to discuss measures to be taken were held between the Chancellor of the Exchequer, Treasury officials and the Governor and other representatives of the City over the Bank Holiday weekend which preceded the declaration of war.[2] The result was a speech in the House of Commons on 5 August (war had been declared a few hours before at midnight) by the Chancellor, Lloyd George. He outlined the plan for the issue of one pound and ten shilling notes and admitted that '. . . after a very anxious discussion . . . there are arguments on both sides . . .' it had been concluded that it would be better to make it a Government note, but he omitted to explain why. On the following day the Currency and Bank Notes Act, 1914 was passed authorising the Treasury to issue notes for one pound and ten shillings, and that they should circulate 'as fully as sovereigns and half-sovereigns are current and shall be legal tender in the United Kingdom for the payment of any amount'. The Act confirmed the convertibility of these Currency notes, or Treasury notes as they became known, and stipulated that the design and printing was to be in the hands of the Treasury. It seems that the Bank initially regarded this appropriation of its traditional note-issuing responsibility merely as a temporary expedient, because the Printing Department was instructed by the Governor to begin work on a Bank of England one pound note based on the familiar design used for the higher denominations.[3] At the same time the presses were labouring twenty-four hours a day, mainly producing five pound notes and postal orders to meet anticipated demand.

The Bank seemed finally to have overcome its nervousness about low denominations – indeed a trial one pound note had been produced some twenty-odd years before as a result of comments made in 1891 by G.J.Goschen,[4] then Chancellor of the Exchequer, in an after-dinner speech.[5] He believed that the Baring crisis would not have been so serious had the gold reserve been greater. In order to enlarge it and so be better placed should such a crisis recur, he advocated an issue of small denomination notes to take the place of the sovereign and half-sovereign; the Bank was in favour[6] and a trial design was even printed but in the event the Chancellor did not follow the idea through. So, when the idea of low denomination notes was mooted in 1914, the Bank did not shrink back in horror; it had already come to terms with the concept. This, and the fact that its proprietorial instincts had been alerted by the vision of others making the running on questions of note issue, led to the speedy production of the proof of a new Bank of England one pound note. It was a masterpiece of design encapsulating over two hundred years of bank note experience.

The florid script was impeccable. Maclise's Britannia was put aside and the one which had preceded it re-used. The masterstroke, though, lay in the reduction of the dimensions of the new note from that of the higher denominations (approximately $5\frac{1}{4} \times 8\frac{1}{2}$ inches; 133×216 mm) to just under 4 by 6 inches (101×152 mm). It seemed to set the note apart from its more valuable relatives – perhaps because the design was crystallised in the smaller note it acquired a coherence that was not so apparent in the others. It was a clear, concise, and beautifully balanced note, but it lost the contest to a far less worthy opponent.

There were two main reasons why the Treasury's note was preferred to the Bank's and neither had anything to do with design or quality; if they had, the Bank's offering would have won hands down. But the Bank, with its insistence on excellence as regards the printing and paper – it was felt that a low denomination note could only be safely issued on hand-made paper – could not have supplied the notes as quickly as the Government required.[7] Furthermore, although originally the aim had been that the Bank should handle the issue, the Scottish bankers had objected. They felt that because the authority of the Bank was not acknowledged in Scotland, low denomination Bank of England notes would not circulate there but that a governmental issue would.[8] So it came about that the Treasury was the issuer of the emergency notes whilst the Bank acted as its agent in distributing them.

The new one pound notes were available for the first time on Friday 7 August: they were poor examples of the printer's art and reminiscent in that respect of the first one pound issue in 1797. The firm chosen by the Stationery Office, to whom the print buying had been delegated, Waterlow Brothers and Layton, had never printed anything in the nature of a bank note before.[9] Surface printed in black on one side only, on paper originally intended for postage stamps, they measured $2\frac{1}{2}$ by 5 inches (63.5 × 127 mm), bore a vignette of the head of the monarch, King George V, and the facsimile signature of Sir John Bradbury, Permanent Secretary to the Treasury. The notes quickly acquired the nickname of 'Bradburys' which persisted even after Bradbury had moved on and a new signature appeared on them. Although they stated that they were '. . . a Legal Tender for a payment of any amount . . .' they gave no hint of their convertibility, whereas the Bank's note had confidently promised to pay '. . . on Demand the Sum of One Pound in Standard Gold Coin . . .'. This clear indication of the Threadneedle Street note's convertibility may also have diminished its chances of winning the contest. The statement was so bold that it was almost an inducement to change the note into gold and this was precisely what the Government wished to avoid: the Currency note certainly side-stepped the issue. A week later the ten shilling note appeared: it was of the same format and quality as the one pound but the printing was in red. The Stationery Office had again contracted Waterlow Brothers and Layton, although the latter were assisted with this note by Thomas De La Rue and Company.[10] Not surprisingly a new design incorporating more sophisticated printing techniques was soon sought, and in October De La Rue's produced a revised one pound note of slightly

The £1 (127 × 64 mm) and 10/- currency notes (or 'Bradburys') hurriedly issued in August 1914 to take the place of the sovereign and half-sovereign.

116

larger dimensions ($5\frac{7}{8} \times 3\frac{1}{4}$ inches; 148×82 mm). Surface printed in black again, but this time on watermarked paper, the portrait of the monarch was retained whilst the designer, George Eve, had added another vignette depicting St George and the dragon. It was a more refined product, and much more of a 'Bank' note than its predecessor. The ten shilling note (printed as before by Waterlow Brothers and Layton) followed in January and was the same pattern as the new one pound although some slight differentiation between the two had been made in the dimensions ($5\frac{3}{8} \times 3$ inches; 136×76 mm). The Bank watched with interest and indeed visibly stiffened when it saw that this second series of Treasury notes was printed on paper with, amongst other features in the watermark, a waved line, but this was not removed until the third series. Whilst the second series was an improvement there remained room for much more.

The third series, designed by Bertram Mackennal, was a well-considered and worthy replacement and represented a great step towards the first officially-issued pictorial note in this country. The one pound denomination was issued in January 1917 and bore two dominant features – on the left, St George and the dragon, based on the Pistrucci design which first appeared on the sovereign in 1817, and, on the right, a reworked portrait of King George V, whilst the back, as if to emphasise the identity of the issuing body, bore a sweeping view of the Houses of Parliament. The ten shilling note, issued some twenty-one months later, also carried the royal portrait, but in place of St George, Mackennal put a standing, helmeted Britannia derived from the Royal Mint examples: the fact that she was not seated and that she held a trident instead of a spear confirmed this. Both notes were printed by photogravure[11] by Waterlow Brothers and Layton, the one pound having brown as the predominant colour and the ten shillings having green.

When the Chancellor, McKenna, was shown the proofs of the new photogravure notes he refused to approve them and asked the Bank to submit a design.[12] His reaction on seeing the miniature note – this time the Maclise

Unnumbered and undated proof of the Bank's proposed £1 design. It confidently promised convertibility into gold coin. (160×95 mm)

Third Series £1
currency notes were
first issued in 1917 and
bore a representation
of St George and the
dragon based on the
Pistrucci design first
used on the sovereign
100 years before.
(151 × 84 mm)

St George and the
dragon. Detail from
the Third Series £1
Currency note.

On the back of the £1 of the Third Series Currency notes the Houses of Parliament were depicted.

Britannia was used — was favourable and he wrote 'I like your design. Nobody can deny that it is a great improvement on ours'.[13] Nevertheless, although Portals could now produce by machine a paper that was virtually indistinguishable from handmade,[14] and despite the fact that the Governor wrote to the Chancellor stating that Somerset House were satisfied 'as to the competence of the Contractors to print our design upon their machinery should you so desire',[15] the idea foundered. All the Bank could do now was to wait. The Court of Directors had minuted at its first meeting after the crisis in the summer of 1914 that should the new notes become permanent their issue should be handled by the Bank;[16] the wait was to be a long one.

At this point it is timely to consider briefly the subject of convertibility. In August 1914 when Treasury notes first came on the scene they, and of course the Bank's own notes, were convertible into gold coin. Although the public could demand sovereigns for their notes they were actively discouraged from doing so by appeals to their patriotism. In August 1915 the Treasury urged the public to use notes instead of gold whenever possible and to pay in gold to the Post Office and banks.[17] Indeed the Bank's own counter clerks had been instructed to tender Treasury notes in lieu of sovereigns and half-sovereigns unless gold coin was specifically requested.[18] However, once the Defence of the Realm Regulations covering the melting and sale of gold were passed,[19] the Bank felt justified in asking for an explanation whenever gold was demanded and, after April 1919, when its export was forbidden, there could hardly have been an acceptable excuse for a presenter to insist on gold; strictly speaking, though, the Bank was acting *ultra vires*. The Bank of England Act of 1833 had made its notes legal tender for all sums above five pounds but it was conditional upon the Bank changing them into gold on demand, and the Treasury Solicitor had pointed out that a note payable on demand is not payable subject to conditions or enquiries.[20] Nevertheless despite the riskiness of the position the Bank felt that it was justified in continuing to act in this way, because it was in the national interest.

In 1925 the Chancellor of the Exchequer, Winston Churchill, announced that the export of gold would no longer be blocked and that this country was returning to a gold standard.[21] But it was to be only a partial return as there would be no gold circulation. The Gold Standard Act, 1925,[22] released the Bank from its obligation to pay its notes and Treasury notes in gold but bound it to sell gold in the form of 400 ounce bars at £3–17s–10½d per fine ounce to anyone who demanded it. The hope was that eventually the reserves would be built up to a level where there might be a full 'return to gold' but it was a vain hope. The reasons were many and varied and beyond the ambit of this work but eventually, inevitably, this country 'went off gold'. The reserves had proved insufficient and so, on 21 September 1931, the Gold Standard (Amendment) Act was passed by Parliament:[23] the new legislation suspended the subsection of the 1925 Act which required the Bank to sell bar gold.

The question of amalgamating the two note issues was never very far from the Bank's mind and in June 1924, following a recommendation from Threadneedle Street, the Chancellor of the Exchequer appointed a committee to consider this.[24] The Committee on Currency and Bank of England Note Issues recommended, and it was accepted by the Treasury, that the Currency note issue should be transferred to the Bank who should be responsible for the production of one pound and ten shilling notes. Definite plans could now be laid, machinery ordered, designs researched, proofed and submitted.

The new Bank of England one pound and ten shilling[25] notes made their appearance on 22 November 1928, the date fixed for the amalgamation of the Bank and Treasury issues by the Currency and Bank Notes Act, 1928: the 1914 idea of a miniature version of the higher denominations had been dropped in favour of designs which seemed to be a natural progression from certain features of the Currency notes they replaced.

At first the notes were of the same size as the Currency notes but of slightly thicker paper; the layout and style of lettering was based on that of the higher denominations except that the date-line was omitted; the Bank's proprietary watermark – the waved line – was used round the edges of both notes and, centrally-placed in a 'window' watermark, a helmeted Britannia looked to the right. The Bank had been assisted in the selection of this Britannia, wearing a helmet of classical design, by the Keeper of the Department

Plate 5

(*Above*) Artwork for the back of the £1 Series 'A' note showing the Threadneedle Street frontage of the old Bank. It was the first issued Bank of England note to be printed in colour. (150 × 84mm)

(*Right*) Detail of the Bank of England £5 Series 'B' note designed by Stephen Gooden. First issued February 1957. This note replaced the familiar white 'fiver'.

Plate 6

Design in pen and ink by Reynolds Stone for the back of the Bank of England £10 Series 'C' note, issued February 1964.

The Battle of Fuentes de Onoro, 1811. Master drawing by H.N. Eccleston for the back of the £5 Series 'D' note. Issued November 1971.

Plate 7

Gouache by H.N. Eccleston of the balcony scene from Romeo and Juliet; used for the back of the £20 Series 'D' note, the first of the Bank of England's new pictorial series. Issued July 1970.

Portrait vignette of HM The Queen from the £1 Series 'C' note designed by Robert Austin. Issued March 1960. The first Bank of England note to bear the portrait of the reigning monarch.

Plate 8

Master drawing by H.N. Eccleston of phoenix used on the front of the £50 Series 'D' note. Issued March 1981.

of Coins and Medals of the British Museum and, as if to vitiate any criticism of this choice of Britannia, publicly acknowledged the help of the British Museum. Again, in common with the higher denominations, the Maclise Britannia was used. Underlying coloured tinting was employed to make photographic forgery difficult; almost 100 years before, Henry Bradbury had pointed out to the Bank the potential dangers of photography in this respect and how it might be countered by colour-printing.[26]

The one pound note was printed in green with an underlying crossbanded tint of blue, whilst the ten shillings was in red with a mauve tint. The design on the back of both, the work of W.M.Keesey, who was also an architect, used a rich pattern of acanthus leaves based on the foliage surrounding the Maclise Britannia. The back of the one pound Currency note had borne a view of the Houses of Parliament as if to identify it as a 'State' issue: similarly the back of the Bank's new one pound note carried a representation of its Threadneedle Street frontage. Furthermore, although the one pound Currency note had not given any indication on the back as to its value, the Bank's showed, somewhat ironically, the reverse of the sovereign.

These designs marked a sea change in the Bank's attitude towards the production of notes, and were the springboard from which other coloured

The £1 (151 × 85 mm) and 10/- (140 × 78 mm) notes issued by the Bank from November 1928 to replace the Currency notes. They were the first coloured Bank of England notes. The Maclise Britannia was used and the designs remained, in use until 1960 and 1961 respectively. These examples bear the facsimile signature of L.K. O'Brien, Chief Cashier, 1955–62.

The back of the £1 Series 'A' showed the Threadneedle Street frontage of the Bank above a swirling pattern of acanthus leaves.

The issue of branch notes ceased in 1939. £50 Bristol note dated 29 August 1918. (209 × 128 mm)

The design of all the Bank's notes apart from the 1928 issue £1 and 10/- was virtually unchanged from 1855 until 1957. £100 note dated 17 January 1938. (215 × 131 mm)

notes and finally those of a more pictorial nature were to be launched. Machine-engraving, which had been suggested and rejected during the inimitable note enquiry, was heavily used for the first time by the Bank; even the predominant colours – the green of the one pound and the red of the ten shilling – set the pattern for subsequent issues. From the Bank's point of view, the success of these designs was evidenced by the fact that they remained fundamentally unaltered for over thirty years, although, of course, there were some changes: printing techniques advanced, different colours were used as an emergency measure and metal thread was introduced in 1940. The ten shilling note was the last to carry the Maclise Britannia which had served on all issued Bank of England notes since 1855. Alongside these coloured notes the Bank issued its familiar white series whose design continued virtually unaltered from 1855 and which was still printed by letterpress from electrotypes. However, in 1943 the Chancellor of the Exchequer announced to the House of Commons that 'to provide an additional handicap to those who may contemplate breaches of exchange control and other regulations' the Bank would no longer issue notes of ten pounds and above.[27] In this way notes circulating abroad could be isolated, and black market operations and tax evasion made more difficult. It was also aimed as a counter-measure to the threat posed by the large-scale forgery operation of this series by the Germans, in the project we now know was code-named 'Operation Bernhard'.[28] The notes were produced by inmates at Sachsenhausen concentration camp and used to finance espionage activities. Various technical problems such as the quality of the paper and the ageing of the notes had been ingeniously solved by the Germans, and the forgeries represented a serious threat to the credibility of the Bank's notes.

In 1957 a coloured five pound note[29] bearing a powerful, confident design exhibiting extraordinary draughtsmanship was released. It was the work of Stephen Gooden who had been the Bank's consultant note designer for over twenty years and yet, of all his visually stunning output for the Bank, only the 1957 five pounds was ever issued. Using the same quality paper (with metallic thread) as that used for the one pound, and using blue for the principal colour, the note bore a striking, helmeted Britannia on the left, balanced by a window watermark of another Britannia on the right: the waved line watermark again appeared round the edge. The promissory clause was placed slightly to the right of centre, and beneath the Chief Cashier's signature St George was slaying the dragon. On the back, a standing lion with a double-warded key formed the single dominant image on a ground of geometrical lines in blue, over a green and mauve background. The key represented the traditional dual responsibility of the Bank, to protect and secure the nation's treasure and, when necessary, to release it, whilst the lion symbolising strength, is, by custom, the guardian of treasure houses.

The first coloured £5 note (Series 'B') issued by the Bank. Designed by Stephen Gooden it was a radical departure from the traditional design. The predominant colour, blue, has been used for this denomination ever since. (158 × 90 mm)

The back of the Series 'B' £5 showing a lion with double-warded key.

The Series 'C' designed by
Robert Austin was the first Bank of
England note to bear the monarch's
portrait. Issued 1960.
(151 × 72 mm)

Detail from the back of the Series 'C' £1.

Primarily issued because of the better protection afforded by colour-printing, this aesthetically-pleasing note was released on 21 February 1957; the issue of the then existing five pound note – the last of the familiar series of white notes – ceased from that day although the two designs circulated alongside each other whilst the new replaced the old as the latter became unfit for circulation.

The Gooden five pound note seems to have served as a bridge between Keesey's pre-war small denomination notes and a full-blown pictorial series. A better choice could hardly have been made. It is almost as if the Gooden note was intended to give the public a taste of and for pictorial notes and thereby to wean them off the Bank's traditional black on white design which was comfortably familiar.

In March 1960 a new one pound note, the work of Gooden's successor, Robert Austin, was announced. It was to be the first of a new series[30] and broke with tradition in two ways: it was to be the first Bank of England note to bear the portrait of the reigning monarch, and the watermark (this, too, was Austin's work), a continuous pattern of classical profiles, omitted the waved-line design used by the Bank for more than 150 years. This change in watermark design foreshadowed the introduction of printing machinery fed by a continuous reel of paper on which it was not feasible to align, as previously, both print and watermark. The note was designed so that it could be printed by the existing sheet-fed machines as well as by the new.

Although it had been originally intended that the new series consisting of four denominations – ten shillings, one pound, five pounds and ten pounds – should be identical in size, after representations had been made from the blind, it was decided that the denominations should increase in size as they did in value. The long-serving Maclise Britannia was dropped in favour of a much more modern looking lady. The new note[31] was smaller than the one it replaced and continued the custom of using green for the one pound denomination.

The second note in the series, the ten shilling, came out in October 1961. Again designed by Robert Austin, there were several features common to both notes: the royal portrait and new Britannia appeared on the front of each whilst on the backs the same Britannia was centrally placed. (With the departure of the Maclise Britannia the last link with the 1855 issue was broken.) Both designs used complicated machine-engraving particularly on the back where, however, the right hand side was kept mainly free of printing in order to leave the watermark unobscured. As to colour, the ten shilling note was reddish-brown, broadly following (as had the one pound note) the hue of its predecessor. To sum up, these new designs were necessary so that new printing techniques could be employed to reduce the cost of production and increase output because of the ever-

The Series 'C' 10/-, again the work of Robert Austin, was issued in October 1961. (140 × 66 mm)

As with the £1 the main feature on the back of the Series 'C' 10/- was a new representation of Britannia.

increasing number of notes in circulation. The old Keesey-designed notes had remained virtually unchanged since 1928 and could not be printed by the new methods.

The next note in the series – for five pounds – followed in February 1963, six years to the day that the Gooden note had appeared. The designer was Reynolds Stone although strictly speaking he did not replace Robert Austin because, when the latter resigned in 1961, both were working for the Bank on note design on a consultancy basis. Reynolds Stone's forte lay in lettering – he had learnt from Eric Gill – and, after reading history at Magdalene College, became an unofficial apprentice studying printing at the Cambridge University Press.[32] Later he moved on to boxwood engraving, a medium in which he grew masterly and to which he resorted when confounded by the seemingly insoluble problems of note design. The great glory of the two

February 1963 saw the
appearance of a new £5
note (Series 'C') designed
by Reynolds Stone.
(140 × 84 mm)

On the back of the
series 'C' £5 Reynolds
Stone depicted a new
Britannia for which his
daughter was the model.

Series 'C' £10 by
Reynolds Stone. First
issued 1964. Predominant
colour, brown.
(150 × 93 mm)

notes Stone designed – the five pound already mentioned and the ten pound issued in 1964 – lies in their lettering which is timeless. He created a new portrait of HM The Queen and this appeared on both notes which, like the others in the series, were embellished with machine-engraving. The five pound note, which was blue, carried a new version of Britannia on the back for which the designer's daughter was the model; a smaller version of this Britannia appeared on the front of the ten pound note, whilst on the back Gooden's theme of a lion and double-warded key is echoed but by using a rather more stylised lion. With the ten pound note one important change was introduced to this series: for the first time the watermark consisted of a portrait of HM The Queen, and it was possible to do this because the design was intended to be plate-printed in sheets, and not to be produced on the new reel-fed machinery. The colour chosen for this denomination, which had not been issued since 1943, was brown.

In March 1968 a new series[33] of Bank of England notes was announced. There were several reasons for it: it had become clear that the issue of ten shilling notes would have to cease[34] and that a twenty pound note would have to be introduced. The opportunity could be taken to rationalise and reduce the sizes generally to allow for the addition and thereby to economise on the amount of paper needed. Also, improved protection against forgery could be introduced through the latest design and printing technology.

The new series was to have several specific design features and concepts: a new portrait of HM The Queen on the front of each note, a new design for Britannia, and on each reverse the representation of a famous historical figure who had contributed to this country's national life. The whole series of five denominations – one, five, ten, twenty and fifty pound notes – was the work of one designer, H. N. Eccleston. In this way a coherent and integrated overall structure for the series was achieved.

In July 1970 the twenty pound note heralded the start of this new series. The portrait of HM The Queen is not totally enclosed, and this aspect of the royal portrait sums up yet another concept embodied in each denomination, namely that picture blends into background and back to picture again. There are no clear boundaries. On the front a striking, individualistic example of St George and the dragon appears, and on the back William Shakespeare, drawn from the memorial statue in Westminster Abbey, is depicted; behind him Eccleston gives us his conjectural version of the balcony scene from *Romeo and Juliet*. Although the note is predominantly purple on both front and back, its general background is composed of multi-colour patterns containing gold, blue and green tints. In 1984 two significant changes were made to this note: through a process known as 'windowing' the security thread was made to appear at intervals on the surface of the note. The second change concerned the watermark which originally depicted HM The Queen and was changed to one portraying Shakespeare. This was because it was felt

The first of the new pictorial notes, the Series 'D' £20 was issued in July 1970. Purple. By H.N. Eccleston, the Bank's first full-time Artist-Designer. (90 × 160 mm)

The royal portrait from the front of the Series 'D' £20.

Series 'D' £5. Issued November 1971.
Blue. By H.N. Eccleston. (78 × 146 mm)

Detail of the royal portrait from the £5
'D' showing HM The Queen in the robes of
the Order of the Garter.

Pencil and wash drawing by H.N. Eccleston for the Wellington portrait on the back of the £5 'D'.

that the watermark of HM The Queen should only be used for the highest denomination and the fifty pound note had been issued in 1981.

The next in the series, the five pound note, was released in November 1971, and followed its two denominational predecessors by having blue as its main colour. The historical figure chosen was the first Duke of Wellington whose portrait, based by Eccleston on one in Apsley House, appears on the back of the note alongside a battle scene based on the Battle of Fuentes de Onoro which had taken place during the Peninsular Campaign. The central vignette on the front shows a delicately-drawn Winged Victory, a particularly popular symbol at that time of military prowess, whilst the general background of the note is made up of tinted patterns mainly of gold, blue and red. The

Winged Victory on the front of the
£5 'D' relates to the battle scene from the
Peninsular War on the back and the
Wellington portrait.

Britannia on the front of the £5 'D'.

133

£10 Series 'D'.
Issued February 1975.
Designed by H.N. Eccleston.
Predominant colour, brown.
The same portrait as on the
£20 'D' of HM The Queen in
state robes.
The central vignette shows a
lily symbol used by Florence
Nightingale.
(85 × 151 mm)

Master drawing by
H.N. Eccleston for the
Florence Nightingale
portrait on the back of
the £10 'D'.

method of printing was changed in 1973 from the usual sheet-fed plate presses to the 'Web' process. Intaglio was used on the front and offset lithography on the back which was marked with the letter 'L' to denote the change.

The ten pound note uses the same portrait of HM The Queen in State Robes as on the twenty pound note; the main design is printed in brown while multi-coloured patterns of orange and brown tints cover the rest of the note. A portrait of Florence Nightingale, a blend of images from three photographs, appears on the back with, in the background, a scene showing her ministering to the sick in the Barracks Hospital at Scutari. The lily symbol on the front is one that she is said to have used.

The lowest denomination in the series, the one pound note, was printed in green by offset lithography and had the same portrait of HM The Queen as the five pound note. The design of the vignette on the front which includes a caduceus, cornucopia and olive branch, is taken from a token commemorating Sir Isaac Newton. The note had only one serial number which was located at

£1 Series 'D'.
Issued February 1978.
Green.
Designed by
H.N. Eccleston.
(67 × 135 mm)

The central vignette contains classical references to commerce in the form of the caduceus and the cornucopia and obliquely alludes to Sir Isaac Newton's connection with money in his role as Master of the Mint.

The back of the £1 'D' with a portrait of Sir Isaac
Newton, his reflecting telescope and machine-engraved
patterns suggesting the solar system.

Gouache by H.N. Eccleston for the Newton portrait on
the back of the £1 'D'. Note the apple blossom in the
background.

the bottom on the right; the space at the top left of the note where the number would have been repeated was left blank so that, if necessary, encoding marks could be applied there for use with note-sorting equipment. Newton's portrait on the back showed him seated, with a copy of his book *Principia* or *Mathematical Principles of Natural Philosophy and System of the World* open at the page concerned with the elliptical movement of the planets. The remainder of the back consisted of a machine-engraved pattern suggesting the solar system. This design when first issued in 1978 was printed entirely by the offset method on a sheet-fed machine but from 1981 the reel-fed 'Web' process printed the front by intaglio and the back by offset lithography. The intaglio printing, being perceptible to the touch, gave the note more of the traditional feel of a Bank note thereby making it more acceptable to the public. It ceased to be issued early in 1985. It is perhaps ironic that the note bore a portrait of Sir Isaac Newton who was for nearly thirty years Master of the Mint, and it is the Mint which produced the coin which supplanted the note.

The crowning glory of the series is the fifty pound note: its design and execution drew on all the experience gained from the research and development which went into the other notes in the series. As with the ten and twenty pound notes this denomination had last been issued in April 1943 but the former had been reintroduced in 1964 and the latter in 1970 and the growth in demand for these notes had led to great savings in production: the fifty pound note was to be the key to yet more economies.

In common with the other notes in the series this note carries a portrait of HM The Queen in State Robes, the one used on both the ten and twenty pound notes. One striking feature is the absence of a single or dominant colour: the portrait and rest of the main front design, which incidentally is intaglio printed, are multi-colour – olive green, brown and grey. The rest of the front, which is offset printed, depicts design features of St Paul's Cathedral whilst 'a phoenix arising from the flames' is contained within the central vignette in glowing shades of orange. The portrait on the back is of Sir

£50 Series 'D'.
Issued March 1981.
Multi-coloured, olive green, brown and grey. The central vignette, the phoenix arising or reborn from the flames, is based on a design by Sir Christopher Wren whose portrait appears on the back. Designed by H.N. Eccleston. (95 × 169 mm)

Christopher Wren and was specially created by Eccleston from contemporary portraits by J.B.Clostermann and Sir Godfrey Kneller. The background to Wren's portrait is based on a mid-eighteenth-century engraving of a view of St Paul's from the river. Roger Withington, Eccleston's assistant and now, since the latter's retirement, the Bank's Artist Designer, drew the St Paul's vista which, together with the features of St Paul's and the portrait of Wren are printed in multi-coloured intaglio, the rest by offset. The metallic security

Master portrait of Sir Christopher Wren by H.N. Eccleston for the back of the £50 'D'. Created from contemporary portraits by J.B. Clostermann (1695) and Sir Godfrey Kneller (1711).

138

FIFTY POUNDS

50 POUNDS

Detail of the back of the £50 'D' showing Wren's masterpiece, St Paul's Cathedral. Based on a mid-18th century engraving. The denomination guilloche is derived from a Grinling Gibbons carving in the Cathedral. Wren's interest in astronomy is represented by the patterns in the sky and a section from Flamsteed's *Atlas Coelestis* of 1729. The names of constellations are worked into the patterning.

thread is wider than the threads used in other denominations and has one edge contoured (which may face to either side) in a regular pattern. It is produced on microprocessor-controlled laser slitting equipment made by the UK Atomic Energy Authority.

The might of design

One of the first decisions made by the Court of Directors at their meeting a few hours after the Charter had been sealed and the Bank legally came into existence (27 July 1694), concerned how receipts would be given for deposits, and as we have seen, one of the three methods decided upon – the running cash note – developed into the modern bank note. In the issue of these receipts the Bank drew on the experience of the goldsmiths, those proto-bankers who had been issuing such promissory notes since the middle of the seventeenth century, and in so doing adopted a design of note that was, although influenced by the effects of forgery, legislation, wars, financial crises and advances in printing and paper technology, remarkably long-lived:

despite the refinements and alterations caused by all these diverse factors the fundamental design endured, staggeringly, until the middle of this century. But the great change in the Bank's policy regarding note design came in 1928 with the introduction of its first colour-printed notes, which paved the way for today's pictorial issues. When that step was taken – from words to pictures – note design could move from a passive role to a rather more aggressively positive one.

First and foremost bank note design is aimed at producing a note that is as secure as possible against forgery; in order to maintain that position, full advantage has to be taken of the latest techniques and technology which can touch on any aspect of bank note production. But the introduction of new technology or techniques often demands, as has been demonstrated, a new design; for example the 'Web' machines required stronger paper which in its turn was less receptive to the printing process; also, with these machines, print and watermark could no longer be aligned and so a continuously watermarked paper had to be provided by Portals. The implications of even a simple straightforward change to using more advanced technology can be enormous.

The designer has to work within certain constraints: the note has to be produced economically, since its cost comes out of the public purse; it has to be possible to produce it speedily, because of the quantities required; and lastly it should be pleasing to look at and therefore more readily accepted by the public. But subordinate to all these is the fact that the design should be such that forgeries can be recognised by the public at a casual glance. The public are, more often than not, notoriously lax in examining the notes they receive, nevertheless they are, after all, the first and best defence in the fight against forgery.

The future for bank notes looks optimistic despite the advent of 'plastic money', a term which can be interpreted, not necessarily incorrectly, as being as pejorative today as the description 'paper money' was during the eighteenth century. There will always be people who prefer to use notes, and one only has to look at the popularity of cash dispensing machines to appreciate that. Notes are somewhat more tangible than plastic: those who have handled the white 'fiver' recall, nostalgically, the crackle of the rag-based paper, and the dignity and distinction of the lettering – 'You felt you had something when you had one of those in your wallet' is a familiar cry. Similar comments about credit cards or cheques are, unsurprisingly, never heard.

Today's notes will never achieve that status because, of course, they will not be in existence for as long as the white 'fiver'. Nevertheless, with the depth of research and care that is embodied in their design, with the quality of paper and print used, they compare with the best of the art of bank note design and production, a specialised and highly-developed branch of industrial design which in this country can truly be said to have come of age. Perhaps the public should remember Sir Christopher Wren's exhortation '*Si monumentum requiris, circumspice*'[35] and relate it specifically to those pieces of paper representing the commodity that is said to make the world go round.

New perspectives

For the profession of banking, as for many other businesses, the twentieth century has been characterised by amalgamations and centralisation. The Bank Charter Act of 1844 did not result (nor was it intended to) in an overnight reduction in the number of banks, or of different notes in circulation. But these were the long term effects: by the end of the First World War in 1918, successive amalgamations had created the four big non-note-issuing clearing banks still existing in England today; three years later the last private English bank notes were issued by Fox Fowler and Company of Somerset, the only remaining country bank. In 1845 similar conditions for regulating banks and note issue to those of the 1844 Act were applied to Scotland and Ireland. Because both these countries had a more diffuse system of banking than England, without a public state bank, it was not practicable to limit the right of note issue to only one institution, and a number of banks retained this privilege. But here, too, the long-term trend has been towards larger-scale operations by fewer banks, and only three banks in Scotland, four in Northern Ireland, and the Central Bank in the Irish Republic, now issue their own notes. The same process of centralisation has occurred in the Isle of Man and the Channel Islands of Jersey and Guernsey, where in each case numerous private bank notes have been replaced by a Government issue.

One obvious contrast, therefore, between twentieth-century notes and their predecessors, is the lack of diversity of designs. As the number of banks has fallen and our use of paper money has grown, we have become accustomed to seeing the same few notes over and over again. Furthermore, notes from banks other than the Bank of England generally remain within their own country of issue, and many people are unaware of such varieties as do exist. Inevitably, the consequence is the contempt and lack of appreciation born of over-familiarity. At best we simply take current bank notes for granted; at worst we compare them unfavourably with the elegance and fine workmanship of some earlier issues.

That is a pity, for in fact a second outstanding feature of modern notes is the skill and complexity of their design and production. As the number of notes needed for circulation has grown from thousands to millions, it has become more essential than ever to combine the best anti-forgery security devices with remarkable speeds of production. First-class hand-drawing and engraving, reproduced by intaglio printing and enhanced by machine-engraved patterns, remains one of the best deterrents against forgery, while modern technology provides the means for accurate and fast reproduction. A natural consequence of the change in the structure of banking and note issue has been an equivalent specialisation in security-printing. For printers, as for banks, mergers and expansion have resulted in a few large firms, concentrating on bank notes and other security documents. Of course this is consistent with trends in all areas of printing, as the scale of twentieth-century demand requires enormous capital investment in finance and machinery. This degree of specialisation is very different from the situation in the nineteenth century when bank notes were produced by numerous different engravers and printers, but the results, combining art, craft and technology in a harmonious and secure design, would surely have won the admiration of the early Victorians.

The most dramatic change to occur in the design of bank notes in the twentieth century is the switch in emphasis from words to pictures. With the exception of a few heavily-ornamented Scottish and provincial notes, most nineteenth-century notes gave pride of place to the text – the name of the

An unissued early 20th-century £5 note of the Wilts and Dorset Banking Company Limited, with a traditional early 19th-century style.
CM 1981–11–22–679.
(191 × 110 mm)

The last English provincial bank notes were issued in 1921 by Fox, Fowler & Co., Somerset. This £5 note has the formal design of an 18th-century note.
CM 1980–11–30–438.
(203 × 128 mm)

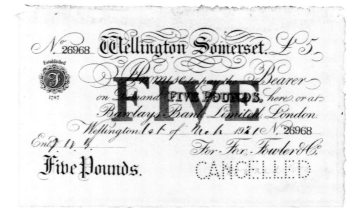

bank and the conditions of payment – with vignettes and ornament used in a secondary, decorative role. Today's bank notes are overwhelmingly pictorial, with the minimum of wording subordinated to an overall design of representational artwork and abstract security printing.

It is interesting and perhaps some vindication of the Bank of England's faith in a familiar and conventional note that so many of the English provincial banks which survived into the twentieth century stayed with the traditional style. A five pound note of the Wiltshire and Dorset Banking Company Ltd carries the time-honoured shield in oak and olive branches, the value printed in blue in the centre, and a sum piece of shaded lettering on a beaded black ground, which dates back a hundred years. In 1909 Stuckey's Banking Company maintained a black-and-white note with blue machine-ruled ovals almost unchanged from the year 1826, when Vincent Stuckey established one of the earliest country joint-stock banks in England. Admittedly the back of the note is quite heavily decorated with black and red security printing, but even this is in the style of the compound plate technique practised by Congreve, Ibbetson, and others in the 1820s. The last English provincial issues, by Fox Fowler and Company in 1921, are possibly the most old-fashioned in appearance, adorned only with eighteenth-century flourishes on the place name heading, one initial in a restrained scroll frame, and the value printed in blue. On the back were dense decorative panels of machine patterns and tiny lettering, again following a style introduced a century before.

Whatever the attraction of this simple, formal style, it could not remain adequate in the new century, on grounds either of security or aesthetic appeal. The change in bank note design, as in so many facets of British life, came with the First World War. Bertram Mackennal's George and dragon for the Treasury notes, based on Pistrucci's design for the sovereign in 1817, occupied fully one third of the face of the note – a suggestion which, it may be remembered, had been made by Beaumont in 1818. The pictorial images were printed in muted shades of green and brown, and showed the Houses of Parliament on the back. Another departure from tradition lay in the size of the notes, which were significantly smaller than earlier one pound notes.

Each of these factors – a large graphic element, soft blended colours, and small size – would on its own have altered the appearance of paper money quite considerably; together they effected a transformation. That it was not simply a short-term emergency measure for war-time was clear when in 1928 the new Bank of England one pound and ten shilling notes appeared, incorporating all three features. In the previous year all the Scottish note-issuing banks had agreed to adopt the new smaller size for one pound notes.

Design and production

As in the past, the choice of designs on bank notes reflects the need for security and to give the bank a clear identity. These needs have been met by a combination of fresh approaches and the re-interpretation of traditional themes in a modern idiom. The blend of old and new arises partly from the way in which designs are chosen: the bank will specify features which must be included; an artist or graphic designer will prepare the initial sketches, after detailed research; and the printers will recommend the necessary security elements.

Innovative ideas may come from any party, but particularly perhaps the printers as they must keep abreast of the latest anti-forgery devices. The use of colour in the continuing battle against photography is a case in point: as that art itself progressed from black-and-white to colour prints, the simple colour-printing recommended for bank notes in the mid-nineteenth century ceased to offer effective protection. That was well proved to the Scottish banks, many of whom did issue coloured notes, when in 1866 the Union Bank of Scotland's black and green notes were forged by a Glasgow photographer.[36] Accordingly, the colours on bank notes have become increasingly varied and subtle, especially in the latter half of this century.

At the same time, however, printing and production may encourage the maintenance of existing methods. To some extent this is due to the security printers themselves, for each firm tends to have its own style, which may be recognisable on notes from different banks, and, as in the last century, printers may well offer an existing range of dies, especially for the more general areas of a note, such as machine-engraved borders and medallions. A second, and most compelling, reason for staying with conventional techniques is that sometimes they are simply still the best option. The most outstanding instance is probably the continued reliance upon intaglio printing from hand-engraved plates, which is justified now in words which echo the artists and engravers of the 1820s. Complex geometric machine-work by its uniformity encourages public trust and familiarity with notes, but its effectiveness is limited by its very precision, which means each example is susceptible to being copied exactly by another machine. In contrast, hand-drawing and engraving create a unique product, deviations from which can be detected electronically. Similarly the tactile relief effect of intaglio remains the most difficult form of security printing to copy exactly, because so much variation of depth is possible. On this point it is interesting that today, as before, a compromise must be made to achieve the best quality with sufficient speed and at manageable cost; thus the amount of intaglio printing may be determined by cost, and its depth limited by the use of dry paper, for while damp paper gives the greatest depth, it is generally too slow for modern demand. Nevertheless, the value of intaglio printing is such that many banks will stipulate that a minimum amount be included in each note design, along with other printing methods. This is another way in which modern bankers follow the advice, if not always the practice, of an earlier generation, for their notes are generally produced by a combination of different methods such as hand- and machine-engraving, intaglio-printing, offset lithography, white-line engraving, and relief-ruling.

Some recent colour-printing, too, adopts a principle from the 1880s. It has been remarked that the rather flat shades of blue, buff and yellow found on notes of the Commercial Bank of Scotland and the Bank of Scotland in the late nineteenth century may have been chosen because the weak contrast in tone value would make photographic forgery more difficult.[37] Twentieth-century notes, particularly in Scotland, have often flaunted spectacularly bright colours: the blue, red and yellow of the National Bank of Scotland, and the Commercial Bank's vivid purple one pound note of the 1940s and early 1950s are good examples. More recently, however, there has been a move back to

Waterlow's distinctive security printing on an advertising note *c.*1930 and on the back of a London County Westminster and Parr's Bank Limited £1 note from the Isle of Man, 1918.
CM 1983–1–24–4.
(204 × 125 mm)
CM 1985–7–35–20.
(156 × 114 mm)

softer, more muted colours, which blend rather than contrast with each other. A pretty example is the harbour view on the back of the States of Guernsey five pound note of the late 1960s and early 1970s, predominantly mauve, highlighted with pale shades of yellow, orange and turquoise. Current notes from the Isle of Man, and the higher denominations of the Bank of England follow the same policy, and although the colours used are much more attractive than those at the turn of the century, the reasoning remains the same: muted colours are much harder to copy accurately.

For the artist, as well as the printer, modern bank note design is highly specialised work, and often a full-time job. Even so, it is still the case that established artists are chosen for this work, and so the notes they produce will be marked by their individual styles. This is particularly evident in the changing appearance of the different series of Bank of England notes since 1928; for instance, the elegant lettering and scrolls on Reynolds Stone's notes for the Bank in the 1960s clearly reflect his interest in decorative wood-engraving, which he employed for other work including book illustration. Even notes for different banks, if designed by the same artist, will declare their common origin. In the 1940s and 1950s, Stephen Gooden, a line engraver, designed notes for the Commercial Bank of Scotland and the first coloured five pound note for the Bank of England. The details and elements of composition for the two banks are quite different, but the style is unmistakable, the gryphons on the Commercial Bank's coat of arms showing the muscular, almost sculptural quality of the Bank of England's lion, emphasising the relationship between the mythical beast and a real creature.

A most distinctive series of modern notes, artistically, is that issued in Jersey during the German Occupation in World War II. The notes were designed by Edmund Blampied, a local artist, and are remarkable for their informal style. Making more use of splashy pen and ink washes than precise engraving, Blampied based the front of the notes on a rather free rendering

States of Jersey £1 note, 1942, by Edmund Blampied. The design is an informal interpretation of the traditional features on bank notes. CM 1984–6–5–321. (129 × 84 mm)

of the traditional lettering, while the backs were decorated with a variety of scenes from local life. The notes share common ground with his other work, the farm girl leading cattle on the back of the one pound linking in style and subject with an engraving of a cart-horse grazing in a field. There can be few state note issues in which the artist's hand is so little restrained by formality and convention.

In most cases, though, the artist is creating a customer product, and the appearance of the notes will depend very much on the bank's specifications, which may be a force either for change or for tradition. The notes remain an important vehicle for presenting a public image, and as the nature and organisation of banks has changed, so, too, have some of the subjects for the pictures and vignettes. Broadly speaking, the themes for notes have come to reflect the country-wide branch business of banks. The local references on English provincial notes disappeared as the banks either ceased to exist, or merged with larger concerns, and modern designs have therefore tended to focus on national rather than local themes. Very early in the century, in 1907–8, the Commercial Bank of Scotland paid tribute to its widening area of operations by illustrating its head offices in Edinburgh, Glasgow and London on a new series of notes. Some fifty years later, a press notice issued to launch a new note issue by the National Bank of Scotland shows just how non-specific the choice of design was:

on the back there is an impression of the forth bridge [*sic*], the selection of which has no particular significance beyond providing an immediately recognisable Scottish scene and at the same time a clear layout, which would present difficulties to any would-be forger.[38]

Sometimes a change in banking authority and organisation, whether by legislation or merger, has directly influenced the designs on notes. As has already been mentioned, the variety of note designs lessens with the number of note-issuing institutions. Hints of this appeared even with later nineteenth-century provincial issues, when some of the larger joint-stock banks issued one basic note design, stamped or printed with different city names depending on the branch of issue. In 1929 the Currency Commission in the Irish Free State took the principle of uniformity a stage further. The Commission authorised a new issue of Consolidated Bank Notes, and granted the right of issue to eight commercial banks, extending this privilege to three banks which had not previously been allowed to issue notes. The notes issued by each bank were identical in appearance, apart from the name of the bank. Designed by a committee drawn from Irish galleries and art academies, every note carried a ploughing scene on the front, and different views on the back of each denomination. Just as branches act as agents for a bank, these banks were note-issuing agents of the Currency Commission, and the notes were colloquially known not by the bank of issue, but just as 'Ploughman Notes.'[39]

When two large note-issuing banks have merged, the new note issue has usually incorporated emblems from both institutions. Thus the notes issued by the Royal Bank of Scotland after the amalgamation with the National Commercial Bank in 1969 displayed the new Forth Road Bridge in honour of the latter, and for the watermark, a portrait of David Dale, first Glasgow agent of the Royal Bank. Sometimes these details bear witness to a long history: the Union Bank's ship motif, which survived on the back of the Bank of Scotland's notes when these banks merged in 1955, dated back to 1750 and the foundation of the Ship Bank, which, after amalgamating with the Glasgow Bank Company, became part of the Union Bank in 1843.

In the above instances, the devices of historical significance relate specifically to the banks; however, people and events from the past have also proved a popular way of giving notes a patriotic national identity. This is a twentieth-century trend, often combined with another feature of modern notes, namely, the use of portraiture as a major element of the design. Sometimes these have been distinguished members of the bank, such as Pitcairn and Cockburn on notes of the Commercial Bank of Scotland; more recently figures of national fame have appeared, Jonathan Swift for example on the Central Bank of Ireland notes. Occasionally, national and banking history obligingly coincide: in 1962 the British Linen Bank placed Sir Walter Scott on their five pound notes, he having been a customer of their Selkirk branch and a keen supporter of retaining the Scottish banks' one pound notes in the 1820s.[40]

Historical scenes often appear on the back of notes; an elegant and rather unusual example is the five pound note issued by the Commercial Bank of Scotland in 1947, which carries a view of George Street in Edinburgh in the 1840s, when the Bank's new Head Office was opened there. The most successful and imaginative use of history occurs on current bank notes which combine portraits of national heroes with scenes illustrating their lives. The Bank of England notes with the Duke of Wellington, Florence Nightingale, William Shakespeare, and Christopher Wren may be the most familiar, but the battles of Robert the Bruce, Robert Burns' 'tim'rous' mouse,

The Battle of Bannockburn on the back of a £1 note of the Clydesdale Bank Limited, 1979. (detail) CM 1980-3-27-1. (135 × 66 mm)

and the natives found by David Livingstone provide equally dramatic images for the Clydesdale Bank in Scotland.

New variations on an old theme

While the overall appearance of bank notes has been radically altered in this century, it has by no means broken completely with tradition. Often modern treatment is given to design features and themes which date back to the nineteenth, and even the eighteenth centuries. The preservation of effective printing methods has already been mentioned. One example is the use of white-line work, a technique of engraving patterns of lines in white against a dark background which was proposed for bank notes from the 1790s, during the period of cash suspension, by Bewick, Tilloch and Applegath. In this century it has been a major feature of the abstract security printing by Waterlow, particularly evident on the back of notes of the Westminster Bank in the Isle of Man, and the National Bank of Scotland, and it is still used for small sections of current Bank of England issues. Indeed, all the geometric patterns of machine-engraved security printing, though freer in form and enlivened by colour, are clearly descended from the intricate borders and medallions produced by firms like Perkins and Lizars.

However, it is not only in printing technique, but also in subject matter that modern notes preserve their heritage. The popular topographical views and architectural features of nineteenth-century country banks are easily adapted for today's national banks; a Highland river scene for the Clydesdale

This scene from the back of a Martin's bank £1 note from the Isle of Man, 1957, could almost belong to a 19th-century note. (detail)
CM 1985—7—35—107.
(152 × 84 mm)

and North of Scotland Bank in the 1950s, for example, or the series of Scottish castles on the back of the current Royal Bank of Scotland notes. In these cases the traditional theme is re-worked to suit the modern style, with pictures filling the whole area of the note, but small engraved vignettes have survived well into this century. A black-and-white engraving of a castle and yachts on the back of a one pound note of the 1950s from Martin's Bank on the Isle of Man could easily belong to a note dating back a hundred years or more. However, one of the longest-surviving vignettes must be a scene used on notes of the Northern Bank of Ireland until 1970, showing a plough, a sailing ship, and a weaver at his loom. This is pure nineteenth-century symbolism for agriculture, trade and industry, and indeed the vignette first appeared in the same form, on notes engraved by Perkins, Fairman and Heath for a Manchester bank in the 1820s. Such exact retention of a design element is unusual (the most obvious instance is the Bank of England's faithful attachment to the Maclise Britannia) but the subjects of agriculture and industry have remained popular. Shipping on the Clyde is a recurring topic for Scottish notes, contrasted on notes for the Clydesdale and North of Scotland Bank in the 1950s with an old-fashioned hay-making scene. In a new series of designs in 1970, the Northern Bank of Ireland produced a modern pictorial note, developing the three themes of Perkins's engraving: three separate vignettes depict farm fields and cattle, a modern shipyard, and a machine operator in a textile factory.

Perhaps, though, it is the symbolic and allegorical elements of modern notes which testify most eloquently to the design of their predecessors. Recently the notes of Scottish banks, so often pioneering, have made of symbolism something distinctively modern, by replacing the traditional coats of arms with rigorously simplified logos, characterless and typical of the late twentieth century. But in most cases, symbolism retains a classical flavour.

Highland river scene covering the back of a Clydesdale & North of Scotland Bank Limited £1 note of 1952.
CM 1983–11–9–5.
(151 × 84 mm)

The current ten pound note issued by the States of Guernsey is a charming example: the composition, proportions and colours are unmistakably contemporary, but the subjects echo quite another century – a Britannia and lion again from a Perkins prototype, two gryphons, and a vigorous branch of acanthus, one leaf cradling a tubby cherub reminiscent of notes by Perkins and W.H.Lizars. Even the lettering is decorated with eighteenth-century

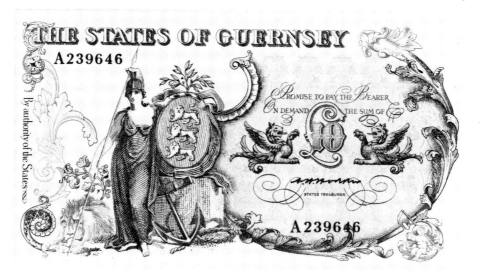

A States of Guernsey
£10 note of 1975 with a
Britannia and lion often
used on 19th-century
English provincial notes.
CM 1980–3–54–8.
(149 × 88 mm)

Britannia and lion
from a 19th-century
£1 proof for the
Macclesfield and
Cheshire Bank.
CM 1981–11–22–345.
(198 × 122 mm)

capitals and flourishes. More often, classical and allegorical motifs are almost hidden amongst the other illustration, as, for example, the triumphant figure of Victory on the front of the Bank of England five pound note, or George and the dragon on the twenty pound note.

In contrast to earlier centuries, bank notes now are such a common-place of everyday life that we scarcely look at them. For the banks this is both a disadvantage and a compliment. It is a drawback because, as the Royal Commissioners realised in the 1810s, public vigilance is a vital force in the fight against forgery. Devices intended to distinguish between the genuine and the false will be of little use if people do not look at notes. On the other hand, our assurance in handling notes arises from our confidence in the banks themselves, and is tacit acknowledgement of their accepted role in modern society.

The powerful and sophisticated banks of the late twentieth century are very far removed from the tentative and often amateur experiments begun some 300 years ago. With increasing maturity, banking has developed a clear identity as a profession, and this is reflected in the notes. We have seen how in the past note design has been strongly influenced by contemporary trends in the arts and sciences. To some extent this still applies, insofar as modern notes are generally designed by artists, and they make use of the latest technology. However, the finished product is not immediately comparable with other forms of twentieth-century art; bank note design is in itself a distinct branch of graphic design.

This distinction is apparent too, in the production process. A modern writer on the history of printing has observed that the current century has completed a trend begun in the second half of the nineteenth century of separating the artist's work from the industrial process of printing. Sometimes banks do follow the modern pattern, appointing a designer whose ideas are then put on paper by an artist for engraving and printing. But often bank note printers have their own artists and engravers, so that while people specialise in different skills, the various stages of production are still concentrated under one roof. Curiously then, one reason for the particular character of modern note design is the debt it owes to its own history, in the design elements, the techniques of manufacture, and the principles underlying both. H. N. Eccleston, the recently retired Artist-Designer for the Bank of England, has defined his work as industrial design to defeat forgery; this is just the outlook and motivation of those artists and scientists who combined in the early nineteenth century to find an improved note in the application of art to commerce. The design of the bank notes of modern Britain is quite distinct both from contemporary printing and earlier notes, but its evolution can be traced in a linear progression through the history of art, banking, and fashionable taste.

Notes

1 The custom of giving notes

1. Defoe, Daniel, 'An Essay on Projects', 1697.
2. Godfrey, M., 'A Short Account of the Bank of England' in J. Thirsk and J.P. Cooper (eds.), *Seventeenth-Century Economic Documents*, 1972, p.708.
3. Richards, R.D., *The Early History of Banking in England*, 1958, p.2.
4. Dafforne, Richard, 'The Merchants Mirrour', 1636, quoted in Richards, op.cit., p.21.
5. Anon, 'The Mystery of the New Fashioned Goldsmiths or Bankers', 1676, in P.L. Cottrell and B.L. Anderson, *Money and Banking in England*, 1974, pp.159–65.
6. Haynes, H., quoted in Richards, op.cit., p.137.
7. Horsefield, J.K. *British Monetary Experiments, 1650–1710*, London, pp.125–8.
8. Clapham, Sir John H., *The Bank of England, A History*, CUP, 1944. Reprinted 1958, Vol.1, pp.2–3.
9. Petty, Sir William, *Quantulumcunque Concerning Money*, 1682.
10. Paterson, William, *The Writings of William Paterson* (ed. Bannister) Judd and Glass, 1859. 3 Vols, Vol.2, pp.63–4.
11. Paterson, William, *A Brief Account of the intended Bank of England*, 1694.
12. Clapham, Sir John, op.cit., p.73.
13. Giuseppi, John, *The Bank of England, A History from its foundation in 1694*, Evans, 1966, p.10.
14. Macaulay, Lord, *The History of England from the accession of James the Second*, New Edition, 2 Vols, 1877.
15. This was the man of whom the diarist John Evelyn had written, after a visit to his Old Jewry mansion in 1679, '. . . this Prince of Citizens, there never having been any, who for the stateliness of his Palace, prodigious feasting and magnificence exceeded . . .'
16. *Court Minutes*, 27 July 1694.
17. Smiths in Nottingham are said to date back to the 1650s (J.A.S.L. Leighton-Boyce, *Smiths The Bankers*, 1958, pp.7–8) and there is a record of an exchequer bank in Exeter in 1696, though its ultimate fate is unknown (see J. Ryton, *Banks and Banknotes of Exeter, 1769–1906*, 1984, pp.116–17).
18. See L.S. Pressnell, *Country Banking in the Industrial Revolution*, 1956, for the origins of country bankers.
19. Checkland, S.G., *Scottish Banking: A History 1695–1973*, 1975, p.23. The Bank of Scotland was incorporated by an Act of Scottish Parliament, hence the reference to the state.
20. Quoted in Richards, op.cit., pp. 162–3. Lord Mansfield was giving judgement in a legal case concerning the ownership of bank notes stolen from a mail coach (see W.

Graham, *The One Pound Note in the History of Banking in Great Britain*, 2nd edition, 1911, p.94).
21. *Court Minutes*, 30 July 1694.
22. Ibid.
23. Ibid, 6 August 1694.
24. Mackenzie, A.D. *The Bank of England Note*, CUP, 1953, p.8.
25. *Court Minutes*, 21 August 1695.
26. Ibid, 7 July 1697.
27. *The Mint and Exchequer United*, 1695.
28. Clapham, Sir John H., op.cit., Vol. 1, p.22.
29. Draft contract (the original has not survived) between Bank of England and Henry Portal for the supply of bank note paper: dated 27 November 1724.
30. Acres, W. Marston, *The Bank of England from Within*, OUP, 1931, pp.121–2.
31. Bagehot, W., *Lombard Street*, revised edition, 1906, p.86.
32. Ibid, pp.89–90.
33. Ibid, p.92.
34. Ibid, p.94.
35. Phillips, M., *A History of Banks, Bankers, and Banking in Northumberland, Durham, and North Yorkshire*, 1894, p.44.
36. *Scots Magazine*, Vol.xxvii, November 1765, p.614.
37. Hall, F.G., *The Bank of Ireland*, 1949, p.54.
38. *Scots Magazine*, Vol.xxvii, February 1765, p.86.
39. Ibid, July 1765, p.388.
40. Philip Hofer in the Introduction to the 1941 edition of George Bickham, *The Universal Penman*, originally published in 1743.
41. Bickham, op.cit, p.4.
42. Ibid, p.8
43. Ibid, p.9.
44. Graham, W., op.cit., p.319.
45. Denvir, B., *The Eighteenth Century. Art, Design and Society 1689–1789*, 1983, Introduction, p.17.
46. Quoted in J. Adhemar, *Graphic Art of the 18th Century*, 1964, p.66.

2 A crisis of confidence

1. Sheridan, Richard Brinsley, speech in House of Commons, 24 March 1797.
2. Greene, Benjamin Buck, Governor 1873–5.
3. *Order of the Privy Council*, dated 26 February 1797.
4. Acres, W. Marston, op.cit., Vol.1, p.276.
5. Poem signed 'Roderick Random', *Black Dwarf*, Vol.2, p.736.
6. Acres, W. Marston, op.cit., Vol.1, p.262.

7. As n.1.

8. Giuseppi, John, op.cit., 1966, p.73.

9. Ibid, p.74.

10. Mackenzie, A.D., op.cit., p.47.

11. *Court Minutes*, 11 January 1798.

12. Act 41, Geo III (c39).

13. Acres, W. Marston, op.cit., p.238.

14. 7 Anne (c 30).

15. Mackenzie, A.D., op.cit., p.6.

16. Ibid, p.8.

17. Ibid, p.14.

18. *Report of the Committee of the Society for the Encouragement of Arts, Manufactures, and Commerce Relative to the Mode of Preventing the Forgery of Bank Notes*, 1819, p.3.

19. Giuseppi, John, op.cit., p.76.

20. *The Gentleman's Magazine*, Vol.57, p.516.

21. Southey, Robert, *Letters from England*. Edited by Jack Simmons, The Cresset Press, 1951, p.122.

22. Greene, Benjamin Buck, *Bank Accounts, Periodical Fluctuations* (B524), p.156.

23. Ibid.

24. *An Account of Plans presented to the Bank for preventing the Forgery of Bank Notes* (B 538), p.30.

25. Giuseppi, John, op.cit., p.60.

26. *Committee of Treasury*, 4 July 1797.

27. In 1818 Alexander Tilloch, then editor of the Star newspaper, reappeared with a new proposal. He had added a coloured engraving to the back of his original submission. When shown Garnet Terry's 1797 copy Tilloch pointed out several indisputable differences, but he had not counted on the prudent record-keeping habits of the Bank for an impression taken from Tilloch's original plate was produced. It showed that the printing plate he submitted as unchanged since 1797 had undeniably been altered. A later report attributed '. . . much of the prejudice which has taken deep root in the public mind' to Tilloch's diatribes against the Bank in his newspaper.

28. *An Account of Plans* etc. (B 538), pp.2 and 20.

29. *Court Minutes*, 12 November 1818.

30. This facility was provided in addition to the Bank Post Bill, which developed from the promissory notes first issued in 1724 and payable three days after acceptance at the Bank for greater security in transit. Post Bills proper were introduced in 1739 and, in the light of the previous fifteen years' experience, were made payable seven days after acceptance. They were issued continuously until 1934.

31. It may be that the promoters of this particular scheme represented the interests of the Spitalfields silk weavers whose industry was in decline because of foreign competition.

32. Bewick, T., *A Memoir*, I. Bain ed., 1979, p.127.

33. Ibid, p.128.

34. Ibid, p.129.

35. Ibid, p.129.

36. Ibid, p.129.

37. *An Account of Plans* etc. (B538), p.15.

38. Interestingly, Reynolds Stone, who designed the Bank's 1963 £5 and the 1964 £10 notes, was also a wood engraver and an admirer of Bewick's work in this field.

39. *Court Minutes*, 3 March 1803.

40. *An Account of Plans* etc. (B 538), p.32.

41. Southey, Robert, op.cit., p.125.

42. *An Account of Plans* etc. (B 538), p.37.

43. This is more than twice the figure quoted in the Society of Arts' report of 1819.

44. *Committee of Treasury*, 19 May 1813.

45. This practice arose out of a legal complication that pre-dated the foundation of the Bank: there had been some confusion over the negotiability of goldsmiths' notes and the position muddied by some inconsistent legal decisions. When the Bank first issued notes the depositor's name or that of the person he wished to pay was written before the words 'or bearer'; but once notes began to circulate as currency it would have been a rational solution for them to have simply been made payable to a fictitious payee. However, the law then declared that the holder of a note, if he were not the payee, could not start legal proceedings in his own name because such notes ie those promising to pay 'AB or Bearer' were not legally assignable. Therefore, from about 1700 the names of members of staff were used until in 1782 it was the name of the Chief Cashier. Seventeen years later his name was printed. From 1855 notes were made payable simply to 'Bearer'. (Of course, these notes for £5 and upwards continued to be hand signed by 'authorised Cashiers' whilst the £1 and £2 notes have the signatures of 'persons authorised to sign'.) It seems probable that the idea was to keep any legal proceedings concerning the Bank's notes in its own hands.

46. Song Sheet 'Abraham Newland'. Libretto by C.J. Dibdin Junior, music by E. Scott. Printed by Longman Clementi & Co., 26 Cheapside, London.

47. *Committee of Treasury*, 9 December 1807.

48. 52 George III (c 138, S.5).

49. *Report of the Committee of the Society of Arts* etc. Published 1819, J.T. Barber Beaumont's evidence, p.14.

50. Southey, Robert, op.cit. p.200.

51. *Court Minutes*, 24 December 1817.

52. *An Account of Plans* etc. (B 538), pp.66 and 67.

53. Ibid, pp.98 and 99.

54. *Committee to Examine plans for the Improvement of Bank Notes, and for the Prevention of Forgery* (B544), 23 January 1818.

55. Ibid, 5 May 1818.

56. *Report of the Commission for enquiring into the mode of preventing the forgery of Bank Notes*. Published 22 January 1819, p.4.

57. *Final Report of the Commission for enquiring into the mode of preventing the Forgery of Bank Notes*. Published 18 February 1820.

58. *Committee to Examine plans* etc. (B 544), 11 June 1818.

59. *Court Minutes*, 11 October 1821.

60. 59 George III (C23).

61. Society of Arts, *Report . . . relative to the mode of preventing the forgery of bank notes*, 1819, p.1.

62. Ibid, p.2.

63. Forbes, Sir William, *Memoirs of a Banking House*, 2nd edition, 1860, p.84.
64. Williams, C.W., 'Considerations on the alarming increase of forgery on the Bank of England, and the neglect of remedial measures . . .', 1818, p.12.
65. Ibid, p.45.
66. Phillips, op.cit., p.84.
67. Hall, F.G., *The Bank of Ireland*, 1949, p.123, n.
68. Private MS, 'John Bliss 1757–1817'. We are most grateful to Mr R.H. Bliss for permission to use this material.
69. *Gentleman's Magazine*, Vol.80, 1810, p.621.
70. Vaux, J.H., *Memoirs of James Hardy Vaux*, 2nd edition, 1827, p.261.
71. Ibid, p.254.
72. Ibid, p.255.
73. Ibid, pp.255–6.
74. Society of Arts, op.cit., pp.13 and 14.
75. Ibid, pp.14 and 19.
76. Ibid, p.45.
77. Ibid, p.25.
78. Ibid, p.31.
79. Ibid, p.57.
80. Williams, C.W., op.cit., p.171.
81. Ibid, p.174.
82. Society of Arts, op.cit., p.42.
83. Ibid, pp.19–20.
84. John Thurston (1774–1822) was originally a copper plate engraver, but later concentrated on producing drawings for wood engraving.
85. Society of Arts, op.cit., p.15.
86. Ibid, pp.57 and 62.
87. Ibid, p.53.
88. Ibid, p.53.
89. Ibid, p.63.
90. Mark Lambert (1781–1855) was a Newcastle engraver who was apparently apprenticed to Thomas Bewick, and later became known for ornamental machine engraving.
91. Society of Arts, op.cit., p.20.
92. Evidence of Vincent Stuckey before the Secret Committee on the Resumption of Cash Payments, 1819, in Cottrell and Anderson, op.cit., p.218.
93. Society of Arts, op.cit., p.11.

3 Tradition and innovation

1. Tennyson, Lord Alfred, 'The Passing of Arthur'.
2. Heywood, B., 'Address delivered at the Liverpool Royal Institution', 27 February 1822, p.11.
3. Quoted in Pressnell, op.cit., p.12.
4. It has been estimated, for example, that after 1822 there were over 400 steel engravers in Britain. See B. Hunnisett, *Steel-engraved book illustration in England*, 1980, p.53.
5. Ibid, p.54, and A. Dyson, *Pictures to Print*, 1984, p.9.
6. Hunnisett, B., op.cit., pp.55 and 69.
7. For a description of the process, see B. Hunnisett, op.cit., p.11.
8. Ibid, p.43. Hunnisett quotes a minimum price of 6d. per copper plate compared with 2s. 6d. for a steel plate.
9. Bewick, op.cit., p.129.
10. Hunnisett, B., op.cit., p.165.
11. *Bankers' Magazine*, Vol. I, 1844, pp.295–301.
12. *Scots Magazine*, Vol.XXVII, January 1765, p.18.
13. 'View of the Progress and Present State of the Arts of Design in Britain', in the *Edinburgh Annual Register for 1816*, Vol.9, Pts 1 and 2, 1820, p.ccccLxxxi.
14. See H. Honour's essay 'Neo-Classicism' in *The age of neo-classicism*, Arts Council of Great Britain, 1972, pp.xxi–xxix.
15. *Bankers' Magazine*, Vol.I, 1844, p.300.
16. Bradbury, H., 'On the Security and Manufacture of Bank Notes', 1865.
17. Ibid, p.5.
18. Ibid, p.4.
19. Ibid, p.4.
20. Ibid, pp.17–18.
21. Quoted in M. Twyman, *Printing 1770–1970*, p.45.
22. Claudet, A., quoted in W. Graham, op.cit., p.323.
23. It is quite possible that they are not Lizars' work, but that his plates were used for later experiments with colour printing.
24. See M. Twyman, op.cit., pp.25–29 on the development and use of lithography.
25. Dyson, A., op.cit., p.7.
26. *Edinburgh Annual Register for 1816*, Vol.9, Pts 1 and 2, 1820 p. ccccLxiii.
27. Thackeray, W.M., 'Caricatures and Lithography in Paris', quoted in B. Denvir, *The Early Nineteenth Century. Art, Design and Society 1789–1852*, 1984, p.81. In this passage Thackeray was comparing English art unfavourably with that on the continent.
28. Hunnisett, B., op.cit., p.43.
29. We would like to thank the military artist Douglas N. Anderson for pointing out this resemblance.
30. Graham, W., op.cit., p.327.
31. Feavearyear, Sir Albert E., *The Pound Sterling: A History of English Money*, 2nd edition revised by E. Victor Morgan, Clarendon Press, 1963, p.235.
32. Feavearyear, Sir Albert E., Ibid, p.234.
33. *Hansard*, 27 June 1825.
34. Clapham, Sir John H., op.cit., Vol.2, p.99.
35. Mackenzie, A.D., op.cit., p.82.
36. Greene, Benjamin Buck, *Bank Accounts, Periodical Fluctuations* (B 524), p.170.
37. Giuseppi, John, op.cit., p.92.
38. Cobbett, W., *Rural Rides in the counties of Surrey, Kent, Sussex etc.*, London, 1830, Vol.II, p.25.
39. 7 Geo IV (c46).
40. 3 and 4 William IV (c103).
41. 7 and 8 Victoria (c32).
42. Paying its notes in this way was equivalent to selling gold at £3-17s-10$\frac{1}{2}$d per standard ounce.
43. Mackenzie, A.D., op.cit., p.86.
44. *Court Minutes*, 31 March 1836.

45. Committee to Examine plans for the Improvement of Bank Notes, and for the Prevention of Forgery (B544), 6 September 1838.

46. Engraving at that time was classified under three headings: Portrait, 'Landskip' and Historical. The last presumably covered any engraving of figures or groups not covered by the first two.

47. Committee to Examine plans etc. (B544), 13 December 1838.

48. Developed from a machine made in the middle of the 18th century, in which a tracing point passing over an object transmitted its movements to a point on a plane at right angles so as to draw a cross-section of the object. It was used for engraving on a flat surface a representation of an object in relief, such as a medal.

49. Committee to Examine plans etc. (B544), 9 January 1839.

50. *Court Minutes*, 24 March 1842.

51. *London Gazette*, 22 December 1854.

52. An electrotype is made by electroplating a thin shell of copper or other metal onto a mould of the original cut or type forme, and then removing the mould and backing the shell with metal. It can then be used for printing. Thus one original can be used to produce a limitless supply of replicas of itself.

53. Mackenzie, A.D., op.cit., pp.17 and 18.

54. Committee to Examine plans etc. (B544), 6 September 1838, p.114.

55. Bradbury, Henry, Lecture on the Security and Manufacture of Bank Notes, delivered at the Royal Institution on 9 May 1856.

4 In pursuit of perfection

1. Hall, Bishop Joseph (1574–1656), *Works*, 1625, p.670.

2. Feavearyear, Sir Albert E., *The Pound Sterling, A History of English Money*, 2nd edition revised by E. Victor Morgan, Clarendon Press, 1963, p.338.

3. Osborne, J.A.C., *The Bank of England 1914–21* (ADM2/3), Vol.3, pp.102 and 105.

4. George Joachim Goschen, a Director 1858–65. Raised to the peerage as Viscount Goschen of Hawkhurst in 1900.

5. Goschen, G.J., Speeches to Chambers of Commerce in Leeds and London, 1891.

6. Possibly for two reasons: firstly the issue of these notes would have brought in considerable revenue at a time when the note issue was not increasing as much as it might due to the growth of cheque banking generally; and secondly because as the 1855 letterpress issue had almost eradicated the problem of forgery there seemed little likelihood of a return of the rampant forgery that had prevailed during the Restriction when low denomination notes were issued by the Bank for the first time.

7. Giuseppi, John, op.cit., p.136.

8. Sayers, R.S., *The Bank of England 1891–1944*, CUP, 1976, p.76.

9. Osborne, J.A.C., op.cit. (ADM2/3), Ch.VII, p.105.

10. Mackenzie, A.D., *The Bank of England Note*, CUP, 1953, p.140.

11. Photogravure: a process in which the image to be reproduced is transferred to a printing plate or cylinder by photography and etched in. The image is recessed into the plate, therefore it is an intaglio process; it gives much better tonal gradations than those that can be achieved by letterpress or offset methods. With high setting-up costs it is generally only used for long print runs.

12. Osborne, J.A.C., op.cit. (ADM2/3), Ch.VII, p.107.

13. Ibid (ADM 2/3), Ch.VII, p.107.

14. Mackenzie, A.D., op.cit., p.146.

15. Osborne, J.A.C., op.cit. (ADM2/3), Ch.VII, p.107.

16. *Court Minutes*, 13 August 1914.

17. Treasury Notice, 6 August 1915.

18. Bank of England internal memorandum to Counter Clerks, 29 July 1915.

19. Feavearyear, Sir Albert E., op.cit., p.351.

20. Osborne, J.A.C., op.cit. (ADM2/3), Ch.VI, pp.4 and 5.

21. Churchill, Winston, Budget Speech, 28 April 1925.

22. 18 and 19 Geo V (c13).

23. 21 and 22 Geo V (c46).

24. Sayers, R.S., op.cit., p.137.

25. Series 'A'.

26. Bradbury, Henry, Lecture on the Security and Manufacture of Bank Notes delivered at the Royal Institution, 9 May 1856.

27. *The Times*, 24 April 1943.

28. Pirie, Anthony, *Operation Bernhard, The Greatest Forgery of all Time*. Cassell 1961.

29. Series 'B'.

30. Series 'C'.

31. 151 × 72 mm.

32. Goodison, J.W., 'Reynolds Stone, his Early Development as an engraver on Wood'. Biographical essay in Exhibition catalogue published by the Dorset, Natural History and Archaeological Society, 1981, pp.20–37.

33. Series 'D'.

34. The issue of 10 shilling notes ceased in October 1969.

35. 'If you should seek his monument, look around'. Inscription over interior of North door in St Paul's Cathedral attributed to Wren's son.

36. The man in question, John Greatrex, fled to New York, but was trapped by an advertisement for a top photographer! See R.S. Rait, *The History of the Union Bank of Scotland*, 1930, pp.299–300.

37. Douglas, J., *20th Century Scottish Banknotes*, Vol.2, 1986, p.46.

38. Ibid, p.108.

39. Young, D., *Guide to the Currency of Ireland. Consolidated Bank Notes 1929–1941*, 1977, p.8.

40. Under the pseudonym 'Malachi Malagrowther', Scott published a strong defence of the Scottish banking system in 1826, following the panic in English banking in the previous year.

Bibliography

Acres, W.M. *The Bank of England from Within*, OUP, 1931.

Adhemar, Jean. *Graphic Art of the eighteenth Century*, Thames and Hudson, 1964.

Anderson, B.L. and Cottrell, P.L. *Money and Banking in England, The Development of the Banking System 1694–1914*, David and Charles, 1974.

Bagehot, W. *Lombard Street*, revised ed., Kegan Paul, Trench, Trubner and Co. Ltd, 1906.

Bankers' Magazine, vol. I, April–October, 1844.

Bank of England Quarterly Bulletin.
1961, pp.24–8.
1969, pp.211–22.
1974, pp.421–3.
1978, pp.359–62.

Bewick, Thomas. *A Memoir*, OUP, 1975.

Bickham, George. *The Universal Penman*, London, 1743. Reprinted by Dover Publications, 1954.

Bradbury, H. *On the Security and Manufacture of Bank Notes*, Bradbury and Evans, 1856.

Brewer, Roy. *An Approach to Print*, Blandford Press, 1971.

Checkland, S.G. *Scottish Banking: A History, 1695–1973*, Collins, 1975.

Clapham, Sir John H. *The Bank of England: A History*, CUP, 1944. Reprinted 1958.

Collins, F. Howard. *Authors' and Printers' Dictionary*, 9th ed., OUP, 1946.

Coppieters, Emmanuel. *English bank note circulation 1694–1954*, Louvain Institute of Economic and Social Research and Martinus Nijhoff, 1955.

Denvir, B. *The Eighteenth Century. Art, design and society 1689–1789*, Longman, 1983.

Denvir, B. *The Early Nineteenth Century. Art, design and society 1789–1852*, Longman, 1984.

Dorset Natural History and Archaeological Society, Dorset County Museum, Dorchester, 1981: exhibition catalogue *Reynolds Stone*.

Douglas, J. (completed by Robert W. Pringle), *Twentieth-Century Scottish Banknotes*, vol.2, Banking Memorabilia, 1986.

Dyer, J.C. *Specimens and Descriptions of Perkins and Fairman's Patent Siderographic Plan to Prevent Forgery . . . of Bank Notes*. Not published. Only 60 copies printed. London, 1819.

Dyson, Anthony. *Pictures to Print. The nineteenth century engraving trade*, Farrand Press, 1984.

Edinburgh Annual Register (for 1816), vol. IX, parts I and II, Edinburgh, 1820.

Feavearyear, Sir Albert E. *The Pound Sterling: A History of English Money*, 2nd ed. revised by E. Morgan, Clarendon Press, 1963.

Forbes, W. *Memoirs of a Banking-House*, 2nd ed., W. and R. Chambers, 1860.

Gentleman, David. *Design in Miniature*, Studio Vista, 1972.

Gilbart, James W. *The Principles and Practice of Banking*, G. Bell and Sons, 1873.

Giuseppi, J.A. *The Bank of England. A History from its Foundation in 1694*, Evans, 1966.

Graham, William. *The One Pound Note in the History of Banking in Great Britain.*, 2nd ed., Edinburgh: James Thin; London: Simpkin, Marshall and Co., 1911.

Hall, F.G. *The Bank of Ireland*, Dublin: Hodges Figgis and Co Ltd; Oxford: B.H. Blackwell Ltd., 1949.

Heywood, B.A. *Addresses delivered at the Meeting of the Proprietors of the Liverpool Royal Institution, on the 27th February 1822, and 13th February, 1824*, Harris and Co, 1824.

Holden, J.M. *The History of negotiable instruments in English Law*, Athlone Press, University of London, 1955.

Horsefield, J.K. *British Monetary Experiments, 1650–1710*, London School of Economics and Political Science (University of London), G. Bell and Sons Ltd., 1960.

Hunnisett, Basil. *Steel-engraved book illustration in England*, Scolar Press, 1980.

Leighton-Boyce, J.A.S.L. *Smiths the Bankers*, National Provincial Bank Ltd, 1958.

Mackenzie, A.D. *The Bank of England Note. A History of its Printing*, CUP, 1953.

Mackenzie, A.D. *The Later Years of St. Luke's Printing Works*, Bank of England Printing Works, 1961 (privately printed).

Melton, F.T. *Sir Robert Clayton and the origins of English deposit banking 1658–1685*, CUP, 1986.

Penrose International Review of the Graphic Arts, 1982 edition.

Phillips, Maberly. *A History of Banks, Bankers, and Banking in Northumberland, Durham, and North Yorkshire*, Effingham Wilson and Co., Royal Exchange, 1894.

Pressnell, L.S. *Country Banking in the Industrial Revolution*, Clarendon Press, 1956.

Reports of the Royal Commission appointed for inquiring into the mode of preventing the Forgery of Bank Notes 22 January 1819 and 18 February 1820. (House of Commons Papers Session 1819 (2) vol. XI, p. 303 and Session 1819–20 (64) vol. II p. 399).

Richards, R.D. *The Early History of Banking in England*, Frank Cass and Co. Ltd, 1958.

Richards, R.D. 'The First Fifty Years of the Bank of England', in *History of the Principal public banks . . .* by J.G. van Dillen. Martinus Nijhoff, 1934.

Rogers, J.E.T. *The First Nine Years of the Bank of England*, Clarendon Press, 1887.

Ryton, John. *Banks and Banknotes of Exeter, 1796–1906*, John Ryton, 1984.

Sayers, R.S. *The Bank of England 1891–1944*, CUP, 1976.

Scots Magazine, vol.XXVII, 1765.

Society of Arts. *Report of the Committee of the Society of Arts etc . . . relative to the mode of preventing the forgery of bank notes*, London 1819.

Southey, Robert. *Letters from England*. Edited by Jack Simmons. Cresset Press, 1951.

Thirsk, Joan, and Cooper, J.P. (eds.) *Seventeenth-Century Economic Documents*, Clarendon Press, 1972.

Trevelyan, G.M. *English Social History*, Longmans, Green and Co., 1944.

Twyman, Michael. *Printing 1770–1970: an illustrated history of its development and uses in England*, Eyre and Spottiswoode, 1970.

Vaux, J.H. *Memoirs of James Hardy Vaux*, 2nd ed., London, 1827.

Williams, C.W. *Considerations on the alarming increase of forgery on the Bank of England and the neglect of remedial measures . . .*, London, 1818.

Wood, W.A. *The Story of Portals* (privately printed), 1975.

Young, Derek. *Guide to the Currency of Ireland. Consolidated Bank Notes 1929–1941*, Stagecast Publications, 1977.

The following catalogues may also be useful:

Douglas, J. *Scottish Banknotes*, Stanley Gibbons Publications Ltd, 1975.

Douglas, J. *20th Century Scottish Banknotes*, vol. I, Banking Memorabilia, 1984.

Duggleby, Vincent. *English Paper Money*, 3rd ed., Stanley Gibbons Publications Ltd, 1984.

Grant. G.L. *The Standard Catalogue of Provincial Banks and Banknotes*, Spink and Son Ltd, 1977.

Quarmby, E. *Banknotes and Banking in the Isle of Man 1788–1970*, Spink and Son, 1971.

Young, Derek. *Guide to the Currency of Ireland. Legal Tender Notes 1928–1972*, Stagecast Publications, 1972.